THE TRANSCENDENTALIST REVOLT

Problems in American Civilization

THE
Transcendentalist
REVOLT

EDITED WITH AN INTRODUCTION BY

George F. Whicher

REVISED BY

Gail Kennedy

AMHERST COLLEGE

D. C. HEATH AND COMPANY

A division of RAYTHEON EDUCATION COMPANY

LEXINGTON, MASSACHUSETTS

7-87

Library of Congress Catalog Card Number: 68-28802

INTRODUCTION

UNTIL very recently the American tendency has been to regard government as a necessary evil, to be kept as near a minimal level as possible. An influential section of the people has always disliked official interference. Extensive programs of social legislation have been fiercely resented. The motives of political leaders have been distrusted, even when they were honestly working for the public welfare. The best men, it is often said, simply will not go into politics. But perhaps the welfare state is now with us to stay and a good citizen can no longer afford to neglect his political duties. The issue raised by the readings chosen for this volume is whether a man eager to improve the quality of American life can work most effectually through political channels or by some other means. The problem is a perennial one, which vexed men in the age of Pericles as well as in the days of Andrew Jackson.

About 1836 and for a few years thereafter a group of young New England intellectuals fell into a way of meeting together in Concord, Massachusetts, to discuss new developments in philosophy, theology and literature. They were greatly stimulated by the exciting ideas originated by German thinkers and circulated among English-speaking readers in the writings of Coleridge, Wordsworth, and Carlyle.

Generally the group met in the study of Ralph Waldo Emerson, a former Unitarian minister who had left his pulpit in order that he might be free to think and write his own unfettered thoughts. It included other youthful and earnest clergymen such as Theodore Parker of West Roxbury, George Ripley of Boston, and F. H. Hedge of Bangor, but among the members were also numbered the progressive schoolteacher and philosopher Amos Bronson Alcott, the poets W. E. Channing and Jones Very, and a recent graduate of Harvard named Henry Thoreau. Thoughtful women were represented by Mrs. Ripley, Elizabeth Peabody, and Margaret Fuller. The novelist Nathaniel Hawthorne, the journalist Orestes W. Brownson, and several now forgotten figures sometimes attended the highly informal meetings.

The neighbors in fun christened the gathering the Transcendental Club, borrowing what may have seemed an uncouth term from the philosophy of Immanuel Kant. The name, however, stuck, and has since become an accepted label for the New England idealists of this period.

The transcendentalists were deeply concerned about the quality of life in America. A great tide of material prosperity, checked only temporarily by the crises of 1837 and 1839 and the ensuing depression, had overtaken the country. Everything was expanding by leaps and bounds. Virgin territories were being opened to settlement from Illinois to Oregon. Turnpikes, canals, steamboats, railroads were rushed into being. The fur trade, overseas commerce, whaling, the cotton culture of the South, the factories of the North were bringing wealth to a happy nation. It was an era of good feeling, a time when the common man

seemed to be getting his share of creature comforts. Yet sensitive observers
feared that all was not well. It appeared
not unlikely that care for man's intellectual and spiritual nature might be
submerged in the rush for easy riches.
What would be the profit in all this
material advance if it were not matched
by an equal progress in humanity? So
the transcendentalists pondered.

Traditionally the church had attended
to the spiritual well-being of the community. The original colonists of Massachusetts Bay had hoped to found
"Christ's kingdom in the wilderness."
They were energized by the sense of a
God-given mission and held to their purpose by a rigid Calvinistic creed. But
in the course of the eighteenth century
the early zeal had cooled, worldly concerns came crowding in to lessen religious dedication, and rationalistic
thinking sapped the Puritan creed. What
remained then was a formal institution,
the Unitarian church, decorous, tolerant,
and reasonable. It had no burning convictions to prevent men from laying
waste their powers in getting and spending. "Corpse-cold," Emerson called it;
a religion of pale negations, satisfactory
to Boston merchants and Harvard professors, but not to those who still cher-
ished the ancient fire of Puritan mysticism or sought to realize the New
World dream of a regenerate humanity.
And among these were Emerson and
his friends.

They did not approve of the low commercial tone of Boston. Human nature,
they held, possessed infinite possibilities
of development. Man was not meant for
money-grubbing. His moral being demanded a larger share of attention than
it was receiving. But how could a change
of heart be effected? Certainly not
through politics, that sordid arena where
the Jacksonian mob and the slightly more
respectable Whigs squabbled in dust and
heat. Would it not be better to appeal
in a dignified way to man's moral nature
by means of pulpit, school, and press?
Or if a reform of institutions were in
question, why not proceed at once to
the realization, even in a small way, of
an ideally cooperative society? Questions
like these occupied the transcendental
group.

In systematic terms the contrast between "the philosophy of sensational-
ism" (materialism) and "the philosophy
of transcendentalism" was elaborated by
Theodore Parker, whose interpretative
essay on "Transcendentalism" (1876)
has been recognized by recent scholarship as one of the best contemporary
accounts of the movement. Readers who
wish to obtain a vivid sense of what evils
a transcendental clergyman was assailing
and what opposition he was encounter-
ing cannot do better than to consult the
white-hot testament which he composed
as a letter to his congregation and
published under the title of *Theodore
Parker's Experiences as a Minister*
(1859). This moving document is too
long to be quoted here, but the excerpts
from Professor Commager's life of Parker
will indicate that he served a sufficiently
useful function, not by participating
directly in politics, but by making himself through contacts with his political
friends "the Conscience of a Party."

When Emerson, in a lecture delivered
in 1842, undertook to characterize "The
Transcendentalist," he associated the
idealism practiced by his representative
modern thinker with the intransigent
attitudes of Stoics and Covenanters and
other strong spirits down the ages:

This way of thinking, falling on Roman
times, made Stoic philosophers; falling on

despotic times, made patriot Catos and Brutuses; falling on superstitious times, made prophets and apostles; on popish times, made protestants and ascetic monks, preachers of Faith against preachers of Works; on prelatical times, made Puritans and Quakers; and falling on Unitarian and commercial times, makes the peculiar shades of Idealism which we know.

The clerical background and training of the transcendentalists predisposed them to think of stimulating men's minds and consciences by a religious revival such as the Great Awakening that had swept New England a century before. Their strategy was to strike directly at motives, to control men by capturing their imaginations, enlisting their wills, and rousing them to an outpouring of faith. They had slight respect for gradual measures. Society in their view was not something to be continuously molded, but to be abruptly fixed once for all.

Practical politicians, however, do not expect to work by regenerating their constituents. They labor diligently to organize individuals and groups as they find them into parties which in turn may be capable of establishing specific acts and institutions of government. "We the people" place in office the party of our election. Our government is made in our own image. If we are not well governed, we have no one but ourselves to blame. The system is far short of perfection, but after a fashion it works.

At the period we are discussing the two major parties were the Whigs and the Democrats. The former, led by Henry Clay and Daniel Webster, were the inheritors of Alexander Hamilton's political philosophy. They tried by all means to promote commerce and manufactures, and to secure the ascendancy of the moneyed interests, on the theory that if merchants and mill-owners were prospering the country at large would share in their prosperity. They were the party of respectability and the status quo.

Opposed to them were the somewhat nondescript partisans who followed the leadership of Andrew Jackson and his successors. They were Jeffersonian without the patrician touch. To many they seemed a dangerous rabble. But they were clearly a people's party, committed to extending the franchise, favoring the small farmer rather than the speculator in their land legislation, jealous of concentration of financial power in the hands of a few, and determined to make of the national government an effective instrument to protect the wage-earner from exploitation.

As Professor Schlesinger demonstrates in the chapter from *The Age of Jackson* quoted in the selections that follow, the program of the Democrats appealed to a large number of contemporary intellectuals and literary men. Bancroft and Paulding held cabinet posts under Democratic administrations, Whitman and O'Sullivan were active political journalists, and even the retiring Hawthorne was willing to accept political appointments in the customs service, and later as U.S. consul, and to write a campaign biography in support of his friend Franklin Pierce. Only the transcendentalists for the most part, though theoretically in sympathy with the aims of the Democrats, remained aloof.

Emerson freely admitted the claims of the Democratic party to his allegiance. "The philosopher, the poet, or the religious man," he wrote, "will, of course, wish to cast his vote with the democrat, for free trade, for wide suffrage, for the abolition of legal cruelties in the penal code, and for facilitating in every manner the access of the young and the poor to the sources of wealth and power."

Elsewhere in a moment of prophetic insight he declared that the mission of "this rank rabble party, the Jacksonism of the country," might be to establish a national culture on a soundly realistic basis, to "root out the hollow dilettantism of our cultivation in the coarsest way, and the newborn may begin again to frame their own world with greater advantage." But having paid lip-service to the policies of the Jacksonians, Emerson declined to take an active part in the hurlyburly of party politics. Did he thereby, as Professor Schlesinger intimates, fail in his obligations as a citizen of the republic and vitiate his own moral position?

When he was asked by his good friend W. H. Channing, an earnest social reformer, to support the crusade for the abolition of slavery, Emerson replied that he had other slaves to free, slaves to ignorance, superstition, and fear, and though he made his position on the slavery question clear on numerous occasions, he would not devote his entire energy to the promotion of any single reform, however important.

In their relation to politics the transcendentalists were confronted by a double question: they had to decide, first, whether they would try to make the world better by working to renovate man's nature or by organizing to improve his institutions; and second, if they chose the latter course, whether to attempt a gradual amelioration or a drastic and sudden change. Emerson and Thoreau consistently chose the moral rather than the political approach. Thoreau was capable of taking direct political action, as when he refused to pay his poll tax to a state implicated in the waging of an unjust war, or when he rose to the defense of John Brown's integrity of character after the raid on

Harpers Ferry; but ordinarily he asked only that men should refrain from "pawing him with their dirty institutions." George Ripley when he launched the utopian adventure at Brook Farm, and Alcott when he plunged into the uncertainties of the Fruitlands project, were training to achieve at once a model of a perfect society without waiting for the slow process of social evolution.

These experiments in ideal living, though both ended in practical failure, were not altogether futile. The community at Brook Farm, in particular, attracted wide attention and insistently raised the question of whether man's social adjustments might not be drastically improved. Even the short-lived Fruitlands venture, with all its fantastic and amusing extravagances, testified to the burning sincerity with which some men devoted themselves and their families to visionary schemes for the betterment of the human race. A highly successful school was conducted at Brook Farm, while the philosophers at Fruitlands assembled the largest collection of Oriental literature then available in the United States.

We return to the question at issue. Were Emerson and his friends misguided in refraining from politics and making their appeal directly to the hearts of men? Could Ripley and Alcott have served the country better if like Hawthorne they had given a stanch allegiance to party and accepted political duties and rewards?

James Truslow Adams, the distinguished historian, has in a general way questioned the maturity of Emerson's outlook:

If . . . we find his culture a bit thin and puerile, is it not because he himself trusted too much to that spirit of spontaneity, of the "spontaneous glance," rather than to the harder process of scholarship and thinking-through coherently; and if we find him lacking in depth and virility, is it not because he allowed himself to become a victim to that vast American optimism with its refusal to recognize and wrestle with the problem of evil?

On the other hand, Professor R. H. Gabriel of Yale, another highly competent student of social history, credits Emerson with an important service to the American culture of his time:

Emerson impressed the common folk of his generation because he preached a philosophy of individualism that not only seemed to set men free, but to provide them with dynamic, creative energy. He gave the doctrine of the free individual sharpness of definition, causing it to emerge, with the clarity of an etching, from the cloudy background of half-formulated ideas.

Thus Emerson with his transcendental associates may be pictured as an ineffective and fastidious perfectionist. Or he may be described as a fountainhead of dynamic currents that set men's creative powers in motion. Which is the truer estimate of what Browning calls "the man's amount"?

> Now who shall arbitrate?
> Ten men love what I hate,
> Shun what I follow, slight what I receive. . . .

But differences of interpretation are the stuff out of which valid judgments are molded. Each of us is entitled to forge and wield an opinion of his own.

CONTENTS

The Clash of Issues

"Our citizens attend both to public and private duties, and do not allow absorption in their own various affairs to interfere with their knowledge of the city's. We differ from other states in regarding the man who holds aloof from public life not as 'quiet' but as useless."

—Thucydides

"This is what deters me from being a politician. And rightly, as I think. For I am certain, O men of Athens, that if I had engaged in politics, I should have perished long ago, and done no good either to you or to myself. . . . He who will fight for the right, if he would live even for a brief space, must have a private station and not a public one."

—Plato

"I have not yet conquered my own house. It irks and repents me. Shall I raise the siege of this hencoop, and march baffled away to a pretended siege of Babylon? It seems to me that so to do were to dodge the problem I am set to solve, and to hide my impotency in the thick of a crowd."

—Ralph Waldo Emerson

"For the typical transcendentalist the flinching from politics perhaps expressed a failure they were seeking to erect into a virtue. The exigencies of responsibility were exhausting: much better to demand perfection and indignantly reject the half loaf, than wear out body and spirit in vain grapplings with overmastering reality."

—Arthur M. Schlesinger, Jr.

"Moreover, any man more right than his neighbors constitutes a majority of one already."

—Henry David Thoreau

"Consequently, Thoreau had to postulate a (by democratic standards) curious distinction between law and right, with the explanation that one has to have faith in man, that each man can determine for himself what is right and just. Hence, no conflict is possible, so the argument goes, because law is law only if identical with right. Thoreau could not demonstrate, however, that there is, in case the majority is wrong, an objective criterion for assaying the correctness of an individual's or a minority's judgment."

—Heinz Eulau

Arthur M. Schlesinger, Jr.:

JACKSONIAN DEMOCRACY
AND LITERATURE

Arthur Meier Schlesinger, Jr., is Regents Professor of the Humanities at the City University of New York. Formerly a professor of American history at Harvard University, he has also made incursions into the world of politics, the most important being his government service during President Kennedy's administration. In The Age of Jackson he attempted a reinterpretation of the period, disagreeing with the now classic thesis of Frederick J. Turner that major characteristics of the period were due to the influence of the rapidly expanding frontier. He thinks it was social and economic changes in the East and Eastern ideas, many of them directly imported from Europe, which played the predominant role in the fashioning of the Jacksonian program. Yet he contends that in this process a leading group of intellectuals played no real part. As a group, they held themselves aloof — and "for the typical transcendentalist the flinching from politics perhaps expressed a failure they were seeking to erect into a virtue."

HISTORIANS of revolution describe a phenomenon they have named the "desertion of the intellectuals." This is the stage in society when the artists, the writers, the intellectuals in general, no longer find enough sustenance in the established order to feel much loyalty to it. They are filled with a pervading sense at once of alienation and of longing, which, one way or another, controls their work, directly if they are political writers, obliquely and at many removes if they are poets. The age of Jackson was such a period. One world was passing away, while another struggled to be born, and the political battles of the Jacksonians helped set in motion a whole train of changes in other spheres. "The strife has been of a character to call forth all the resources of the popular intelligence,"

Theodore Sedgwick, Jr., wrote in 1835, ". . . It has urged forward the whole American mind."[1]

1

Not all writers were politically active, not even all those possessed by visions of a new world. Some, like Emerson and Thoreau, preoccupied most profoundly with the questions raised up by the change, spent years quietly ignoring politics. But, even with such important ex-

[1] Sedgwick, *What Is a Monopoly?*, 7. It would require another and a different book to show how the literature of the day tried to resolve on the moral and artistic level some of the problems faced by Jacksonian democracy in politics and economics. Much of this ground has been acutely covered by F. O. Matthiessen in *American Renaissance*. My purpose here is simply to indicate some of the direct responses of writers to politics.

ceptions, it is yet remarkable how many of the leading authors and artists publicly aligned themselves with the Jacksonian party. Nathaniel Hawthorne, William Cullen Bryant, Walt Whitman, James Fenimore Cooper, George Bancroft, Washington Irving (until the pressure became too great), James K. Paulding, Orestes A. Brownson, William Leggett, John L. O'Sullivan, John L. Stephens, Horatio Greenough, Hiram Powers, Edwin Forrest, Frances Wright, Robert Dale Owen, for example, were all Jacksonians. As Harriet Martineau observed, the Democratic party included the underprivileged classes, the careerists, the humanitarians and "an accession small in number, but inestimable in power, — the men of genius."[2]

The Democrats were exceedingly proud of their intellectuals. "It is a fact well known," boasted the Boston Post, "that with few exceptions, our first literary men belong to the democratic party. Almost every man of note in letters, — historians, poets, and indeed nearly all who have acquired fame as writers and authors are, as might be expected, favorable to democracy."[3] Van Buren himself offered government jobs to Bancroft, Hawthorne, Irving, Paulding, Brownson and Leggett. Even Whigs complained that the word "Locofoco" ought to be used as the "synonyme of ignorance; and yet that party certainly numbers amongst its leaders some celebrated literary characters."[4] For many this fact was cause for indignation. "Why in this fearful

struggle which we are obliged to sustain," cried Edward Everett of Hawthorne, "is he on the side of barbarism & vandalism against order, law & constitutional liberty?"[5]

Many of the authors regarded a position of political liberalism as an artistic imperative. They felt that the Whigs cared only to preserve the tame, reliable and derivative culture of which men like Everett and Longfellow were faithful representatives. The only future for a powerful native literature, dealing fearlessly in truth and reality, seemed to lie in a bold exploration of the possibilities of democracy. "The vital principle of an American national literature," declared the Democratic Review, "must be democracy."[6] "The man of letters," as George Bancroft told Everett, "should be the man of the people," and his own monumental History revealed how a living faith in the people could quicken, unify and transmute into art a narrative which had heretofore been but dry chronicles.[7] Orestes A. Brownson was even more specific. The question of capital and labor seemed to him supreme: "In the struggle of these two elements, true American literature will be born."[8]

[2] Martineau, Society in America, I, 13–14. Cf. George Combe, Notes on the United States of North America, II, 216: "The Whig party in America claims the wealth of the Union on their side, and the Democrats claim the genius."

[3] Boston Post, October 11, 1838. See also New York Evening Post, August 14, 1838.

[4] Francis Baylies, Speech . . . before the Whigs of Taunton, 3.

[5] Everett to G. S. Hillard, June 21, 1849, Everett Papers. Henry Wadsworth Longfellow charged darkly in 1839 that the Locofocos were organizing a "new politico-literary system." Longfellow to G. W. Greene, July 23, 1839, Hawthorne, The American Notebooks, Randall Stewart, ed., 288.

[6] "Introduction," Democratic Review, I, 14 (October, 1837).

[7] Bancroft to Everett, February 7, 1835, Bancroft Papers. Cf. Bancroft to Jared Sparks, August 22, 1834, Sparks Papers: "A vein of public feeling, of democratic independence, of popular liberty, ought to be infused into our literature. Let Mammon rule in the marts, but not on the holy mountain of letters. The rich ought not to be flattered; let truth, let humanity speak through the public journals and through American literature."

[8] Brownson, "American Literature," Boston Quarterly Review, III, 76 (January, 1840).

2

A first requisite for a literature is a medium for publication. The respectable magazines — the *North American,* the *American Quarterly,* the *New-England Magazine,* and so on — were in Whig hands, and during the eighteen-thirties the need for a monthly journal of liberal sympathies became increasingly pronounced. At this juncture a bright young man named John L. O'Sullivan, who had been running a small newspaper in Washington, appeared with the project of a Democratic review.

O'Sullivan was descended from a long line of picaresque Irishmen whose actual careers remain buried under family legend. His father had lived an obscure life, sometimes as American Consul in such places as Mogador and Teneriffe, more often as master, supercargo or owner of ships engaged in the South American trade. A cloud of mystery hangs over many of his transactions, and he was several times charged with bribery and extortion and even suspected of piracy. One aunt paid a call on ex-President Madison in 1827, dressed as a man and followed by four children, and told a fantastic tale of adventures in Europe and America.[9]

Young O'Sullivan graduated from Columbia in 1831 and began a life of free-lance journalism. He was a charming, gay and rather indolent man, with a sanguine temperament, often disappointed but rarely depressed. Nathaniel Hawthorne, while feeling him to be superficial, very much enjoyed his company, and a sterner nature like Thoreau thought him "puny-looking" and over-talkative but still one of the "not-bad." O'Sullivan's sister (handsome enough to provoke even Emerson to enthusiastic

comment) had married another young writer named S. D. Langtree, and together in 1837 the two approached Benjamin F. Butler with the proposal of a Democratic literary magazine.[10]

Butler, who was given to cultural dabbling and even wrote verse for publication, took fire at the idea, subscribed five hundred dollars himself and urged other Democratic politicians to aid in financing the *Democratic Review.* Henry D. Gilpin also took an active part in the search for backing. Jackson, who had long hoped for such a journal, encouraged the project and became the first subscriber. During the summer the editors approached writers the country over, and in October a preliminary number appeared, with contributions by Bryant, Hawthorne, Whittier and others. (When Langtree applied to John Quincy Adams, the old man testily replied that literature by its nature would always be aristocratic, and that the idea of a Democratic literary magazine was self-contradictory.)[11]

[9] J. W. Pratt, "John L. O'Sullivan and Manifest Destiny," *New York History,* XXXI, 214–217.

[10] Poe thought him an ass, and Longfellow, a humbug — both judgments occasionally having their foundation. Julia Ward Howe, meeting Yeats, in 1903, and noting his fiery temperament, his slight figure, his blue eyes and dark hair, was irresistibly reminded of O'Sullivan. Julian Hawthorne, *Nathaniel Hawthorne and His Wife,* I, 160; Nathaniel Hawthorne, *Love Letters,* Roswell Field, ed., II, 242; Rose H. Lathrop, *Memories of Hawthorne,* 77; Thoreau to Emerson, January 24, 1843, F. B. Sanborn, *Hawthorne and His Friends,* 30; G. E. Woodberry, *Life of Edgar Allan Poe,* I, 353; Hawthorne, *The American Notebooks,* 288–289; Laura E. Richards and Maud Howe Elliott, *Julia Ward Howe, 1819–1910,* II, 319; Emerson to Margaret Fuller, February 24, 1843, Emerson, *Letters,* III, 149.

[11] O'Sullivan to Rufus Griswold, September 8, 1842, *Passages from the Correspondence of Rufus W. Griswold,* William Griswold, ed., 213; Butler to Bancroft, May 1, 1838, Bancroft Papers; Butler to Gilpin, April 24, 1838, Gilpin Papers; Jackson to Langtree and O'Sullivan, March 6, 1837, *Washington Globe,* March 13, 1837; Adams, *Memoirs,* IX, 416; Frank L. Mott, *History of American Magazines,* I, 677–684.

Whatever O'Sullivan's failings, he was an excellent editor. He was assiduous in seeking out new talent, and he quickly made the *Democratic Review* by far the liveliest journal of the day. His authors included Bryant, Hawthorne, Thoreau, Whittier, Walt Whitman, Poe, Longfellow, Lowell, Paulding, William Gilmore Simms, Bancroft, Brownson, A. H. Everett and many more. Politically the magazine aligned itself vigorously with the radical wing of the party. The *Madisonian* described it as a "sort of political hygroscope, indicating the state of the air breathed in the party councils of the ruling dynasty," and even men like Marcy regarded it as an "organ of the administration."[12] There is no evidence,

however, that Van Buren used the *Democratic Review* for trial balloons, and in the end the magazine left Washington when Blair's jealousy denied it a share of the government printing.[13] It resumed publication in New York and remained under O'Sullivan's control till 1846. Its circulation in 1843 was 3500.[14]

In the meantime Orestes Brownson had provided the liberals with another organ in his *Boston Quarterly Review*. The concurrence of motives behind this journal showed the wide front of the cultural revolt. His object, Brownson said, was to support the new movement in all its manifestations, "whether it be effecting a reform in the Church, giving us a purer and more rational theology; in philosophy seeking something profounder and more inspiriting than the heartless Sensualism of the last century; or whether in society demanding the elevation of labor with the Locofoco, or the freedom of the slave with the Abolitionist."[15]

The *Boston Quarterly* thus became a compendium of the desertion of the intellectuals, defending in detail the repudiation of the old order in religion, philosophy and politics. Not only Bancroft and A. H. Everett but George Ripley and Theodore Parker, Bronson Alcott and Margaret Fuller were essential in Brownson's broad purpose. To him the fight was all one, though later the political motive grew more dominant, and it almost seemed, as Brownson told Van Buren, that the review was established "for the purpose of enlisting Liter-

---

[12] This reputation discredited the *Democratic Review* in conservative circles. "Will you believe," wrote George Sumner, from Europe, to a friend in Boston, "that because that article on Greece appeared in the *Democratic Review*, the only review we have which goes to foreign capitals, the review which champions in a moderate way those principles upon which our Government is founded, ... the review which Advaros (Min. of Pub. Ins. in Russ.) hailed as a publication which gave a tone to America abroad, and enabled her to appear with a review not a poor repetition of the poor matter of the English reviews — because that article appeared in the *Democratic Review*, it is trodden under foot, and I am denounced as 'an Administration man.' " His brother Charles had written him that Nathan Hale refused to reprint the article in the *Boston Advertiser;* George Ticknor was "sorry to see it in such company"; Justice Story was "much troubled," but "of course did not speak of it out of delicacy to me"; Professor Greenleaf of the Harvard Law School was "grieved" and reported that it had been "lamented by many people who were prepared to be your friends." "Seriously, my dear George," Charles Sumner wrote, "think of abandoning your leaky craft." George Sumner's response was violent: "God *damn* them *all!!* ... I cannot but laugh, roars of horrid laughter, on thinking of all these things. ... How the demon of party feeling must have crazed the minds and feelings of men whose characters one would suppose firm and high." George Sumner to G. W. Greene, November [?], 1842, *Proceedings of the Massachusetts Historical Society,* XLVI, 359–360.

[13] Mott, *History of American Magazines,* I, 679–680.

[14] O'Sullivan to Charles Sumner, April 12, 1843, Sumner Papers.

[15] "Introductory Remarks," *Boston Quarterly Review,* I, 6 (January, 1838).

ature, Religion, and Philosophy on the side of Democracy."[16]

Less bright and varied than the *Democratic Review*, the *Boston Quarterly* was more learned, serious and penetrating. Brownson's personality pervaded the Journal — he became increasingly the exclusive author — and he endowed it with a vigor and cogency which commanded wide attention. John C. Calhoun, for example, was a faithful reader, and even the impassive Levi Woodbury, Secretary of the Treasury, was moved to exclaim of one issue, "What an excellent number was Mr. Brownson's last! Exhort him from me to give us more."[17] (When Brownson began a few months later to give them more, Woodbury became markedly less enthusiastic.)

In 1842 the *Democratic Review* and the *Boston Quarterly* merged, but not before each had left a distinct mark on the development of American letters. Each journal, on its own level, was the best of its day, and both gained much of their energy, courage and free vigor from their immersion in the political ideals of Jacksonian democracy.

3

A surprising number of writers were themselves active in politics or the government service. George Bancroft, driven ahead by an unstable combination of democratic idealism and personal ambition, became party boss of Massachusetts and later Polk's Secretary of the Navy. Brownson held office under Van Buren and ran for Congress during the Civil War. Washington Irving and Alexander H. Everett were in the diplomatic service.

James K. Paulding spent many years on government pay rolls, first as Naval Agent of New York, later as Van Buren's Secretary of the Navy. This bluff, amusing Dutchman was a stout Jacksonian, if by a roundabout road. A man of obstinate good sense, he disliked the cant of radicalism, but disliked the cant of conservatism even more. His famous satire *The Merry Tales of the Three Wise Men of Gotham* (1826) poked fun impartially at the common law, on the one hand, and the dreams of Robert Owen, on the other. Many brief political essays, bearing the stamp of his gruff irony and hearty common sense, appeared in the *Washington Globe* and the *New York Evening Post*.[18]

Nathaniel Hawthorne was another Democratic pensioner, holding office under three administrations. Unlike Paulding, he was not much of a party journalist, though there was once a possibility of his joining the *Globe* under Frank Blair, and in 1852 he wrote a campaign life of Franklin Pierce.[19] Yet he was not as perfunctory a Democrat as some biographers have insisted. His quiet sense of sin and his hatred of human pride immunized him against the claims of Whig conservatism to moral or political superiority. He was not much impressed by Utopianism either. The current of his sympathies, as expressed in his notebook jottings, ran clear and strong with the plain, solid, common life of the people. *The House of the Seven Gables* embodied massively his conviction of the fatal isolation worked by property and privilege, and his fascination with the rude energies of change

[16] Brownson to Van Buren, April 2, 1838, Van Buren Papers.

[17] Woodbury to Bancroft, November 21, 1839, Bancroft Papers.

[18] See Paulding's letters to Van Buren and to A. C. Flagg in the respective collections.

[19] For Hawthorne and the *Globe*, see Franklin Pierce to Hawthorne, March 5, 1836, Julian Hawthorne, *Hawthorne and His Wife*, I, 134–135.

and reform.[20] The "Locofoco Surveyor," as he described himself in the preface to *The Scarlet Letter*, was permanently marked by that day in 1833 when he walked through the falling shadows of a Salem dusk to catch a glimpse of General Andrew Jackson.

Of all the literary men of the day, however, James Fenimore Cooper has probably suffered the most inquiry into his politics. Because these examinations have generally been carried on without detailed knowledge of the concrete party background, it may be illuminating to reopen his case more squarely in terms of the actual issues of the day.[21]

Cooper was basically an upstate New York squire whose politics were determined ultimately by his sense of the security of landed property. His father had been a prominent Federalist; but Cooper early found Jefferson's views on agricultural virtue and popular rule more congenial. By the eighteen-thirties he was ready to believe that Federalist leaders had actually contemplated revolution and monarchy; and in *The Monikins* (1835) he set forth his famous lampoon of Federalism as the "social stake system."[22]

For Cooper, "the heart and strength of the nation" was "its rural population,"

and the agricultural foundations of the republic seemed to him, as to most Jeffersonians, to be menaced by the commercial community.[23] He was convinced that the "natural antipathy between trade and democracy" was causing businessmen to plot a financial oligarchy. "Most of all," he wrote, "commerce detests popular rights."[24] The history of Britain, fortified by his own experience in France in the early eighteen-thirties, proved the inevitable tendency of business rule toward a moneyed aristocracy. "No government that is essentially influenced by commerce," he concluded, "has ever been otherwise than exclusive, or aristocrat."[25] To his political fears he added the contempt of the landed gentleman for the *parvenu* businessmen. "Of all the sources of human pride," he would write, "mere wealth is the basest and most vulgar minded. Real gentlemen are almost invariably above this low feeling."[26]

These prepossessions, deeply grounded in Cooper's experience, controlled his creative impulses as well as his arguments. The sketches of the Effingham cousins in *Homeward Bound* suggest as vividly as any of his explicit statements Cooper's feelings about the respective effects of owning property in land and in trade. Edward Effingham was "winning in appearance," John "if not positively forbidding, at least distant and repulsive. . . . The noble outline of face in Edward Effingham had got to be cold severity in that of John; the aquiline nose of the latter, seeming to possess an eagle-like and hostile curvature, — his com-

[20] See the discussion in Matthiessen, *American Renaissance*, 316–337.

[21] Dorothy Waples's valuable *Whig Myth of James Fenimore Cooper* has done much to place Cooper's reputation in proper perspective by showing how he was systematically vilified by the Whig press for his political views. Robert E. Spiller's *Fenimore Cooper: Critic of His Times* develops the general implications of his social criticism. Ethel R. Outland's *The "Effingham" Libels on Cooper* supplies basic information about Cooper's feud with the press. All these books suffer, however, from an imperfect appreciation of the radical extent to which Cooper's views changed from 1834 to 1850.

[22] Cooper, *Sketches of Switzerland* [Part First], II, 158; *Monikins*, 74, 82.

[23] For the quotation, see *Sketches of Switzerland*, Part Second, II, 181.

[24] Cooper, *Gleanings in Europe*, II, 177.

[25] Cooper, *Monikins*, 408; see also *Letter to His Countrymen*, 65–67.

[26] Cooper, *American Democrat*, 131–132; see also *Excursions in Italy*, 184–185.

pressed lip, sarcastic and cold expression, . . . a haughty scorn that caused strangers usually to avoid him." What accounted for this differentiation? "Edward Effingham possessed a large hereditary property, that brought a good income, and which attached him to this world of ours by kindly feelings toward its land and water; while John, much the wealthier of the two, having inherited a large commercial fortune, did not own ground enough to bury him. As he sometimes deridingly said, he 'kept his gold in corporations, that were as soulless as himself.' "[27]

Cooper's faith in the land and hatred for the financial aristocracy naturally led him, on his return to America in 1833, to become an enthusiastic supporter of the Jackson administration. He adopted the most radical Democratic positions on all questions but the tariff, and was in particular a staunch advocate of the hard-money policy.[28] The rule of property, he said in 1836, is "the most corrupt, narrow and vicious form of polity that has ever been devised."[29] While he had no faith in the infallibility of the whole people, he had even less faith in that of any part of the people. "Though majorities often decide wrong, it is believed that they are less liable to do so than minorities."[30]

In *A Letter to His Countrymen* (1834) he denounced the whole Whig position as an attempt to pervert the American form of government by construing it falsely on British analogies in the hope of ending up with a commercial oligarchy on the British model. *The Monikins* (1835) was a lengthy satirical allegory, at times brilliant, at times tedious, intended to show in more detail in what danger America stood from imitating the business politics of Britain. In both volumes, in the series of travel books he was turning out and in articles for the *New York Evening Post* he attacked the Whig arguments against Jackson's alleged constitutional excesses. In *The American Democrat* (1838) he even defended Jackson's theory of the right of independent adjudication of constitutionality, as developed in the Bank veto.

In his writings throughout the decade, however, there appears beside the approval of Jacksonianism a mounting irritation with the "tyranny of opinion" in America, which, by *The American Democrat* and his novels of 1837 and 1838, *Homeward Bound* and *Home as Found*, was becoming a major theme. Literary historians have interpreted this complaint as evidence of his discomfort under the pressure toward uniformity supposedly exerted by "Jacksonian democracy."

Before accepting this conclusion, it is essential to understand *whose* opinion Cooper was denouncing as tyrannous. In *Sketches of Switzerland* (1836) he declared, "I have never yet been in a country in which what are called the lower orders have not clearer and sounder views than their betters of the great principles which ought to predominate in the control of human affairs." A few pages later, after setting forth a number of routine Democratic arguments in defense of Jackson's use of the presidential power, he commented that current reasoning on these questions "among what are called the enlightened classes" showed how far opinion had lagged behind facts.[31]

---

[27] Cooper, *Homeward Bound*, 12–13.
[28] See especially *American Democrat*, 163–165.
[29] *Sketches of Switzerland*, Part Second, I, 36.
[30] *American Democrat*, 46.

[31] *Sketches of Switzerland* [Part First], I, 177, 212.

There were, in fact, these *two* public opinions for Cooper — that of "what are called the lower orders," which he respected, and that of "what are called the enlightened classes," which he disliked. Yet Cooper was a careless writer, and he could say, immediately after attacks on the "enlightened classes," "I am aware that these are bold opinions to utter in a country where the mass has become so consolidated that it has no longer any integral parts; where the individual is fast losing his individuality in the common identity."[32] In view of the fact that his opinions were "bold" only among "what are called the enlightened classes," it is clear that in this context Cooper's attack on the "tyranny of opinion" is actually an attack on tyranny of opinion *in his class.*

This is, in fact, the key to his assaults on "tyranny of opinion" in the eighteen-thirties (though not in the eighteen-forties). He would say that if certain progressive opinions were laid before "that portion of the American public which comprises the reading classes," they would have no effect on these classes "on account of their hatred of the rights of the mass"; and in the next sentence he would assert flatly, "I know no country that has retrograded in opinion, so much as our own, within the last five years" — when again he clearly meant, not the whole country, but the "reading classes."[33] "After having passed years in foreign countries, I affirm that I know no state of society in which liberal sentiments are so little relished as in our own, among the upper classes," he would write.[34] But when he began laying about

with invective, he tended to forget the qualifications and to accuse the entire nation.

An incident in 1837 intensified Cooper's fears of the "tyranny of opinion." He owned some land on Otsego Lake known as Three Mile Point, which the Coopers had always opened to the village of Cooperstown as a picnic place. In time the villagers began to regard Three Mile Point as public property, and Cooper's attempt to reassert his ownership provoked violent newspaper attacks. Yet it is again hardly just to ascribe these attacks to "Jacksonian democracy." The campaign against Cooper was conducted by the New York Whig press, led by Thurlow Weed, James Watson Webb, William L. Stone and Horace Greeley, most of whom Cooper later chastised by libel suits, while the Jacksonian press, especially the *New York Evening Post* and the *Albany Argus,* rushed to his defense. "It appears that he is ordained to be hunted down," observed the *New Era.* "The British Whig aristocracy here cry havoc, and their creatures throughout the land echo the cry."[35]

Cooper was, in fact, reacting against a pressure toward uniformity, but it was the pressure, not of mass opinion, but of class opinion. It becomes nonsense to say that Cooper revolted against Jacksonian democracy because of its tyranny over opinion, when actually such tyranny over opinion as he experienced in the eighteen-thirties was provoked in great part by his expression of views favorable to Jacksonian democracy.

Cooper's bitter reaction was reflected in the detailed indictment of public opinion he drew up in *The American Democrat* (1838). But the very points at which he chose to attack public opinion as tyrannous were precisely the points

[32] *Ibid.,* 212.

[33] *Sketches of Switzerland,* Part Second, II, 189–190.

[34] Cooper to Bedford Brown, March 24, 1838, *Historical Papers Published by the Historical Society of Trinity College,* VIII, 2.

[35] *New Era,* June 4, 1840.

where, as he considered, Whig editors had improperly meddled in his private affairs, and on every current issue discussed he resolutely took the Democratic side. His novels of this period set forth these same emotions. *Home as Found,* though artistically less expert than *Homeward Bound,* was particularly revealing. Like *The American Democrat,* it had two pervading revulsions: on the one hand, the self-constituted aristocracy of the American Whigs, with their pretensions and snobberies, their servility toward the British, their hatred of "that monster" General Jackson and their scorn for the lower classes; on the other, the menace of the democratic demagogue.[36]

But the fear of the democratic demagogue did not shake his allegiance to the Democratic party. In New York, in any case, as the Seward-Weed policy gained adherents, the most objectionable demagogues mouthing democratic professions were on the Whig side. "The present political struggle, in this country," he wrote in 1838, "appears to be a contest between men and dollars."[37] The Whig victory of 1840 seemed to him, in his pessimistic later years, "little more than the proof of the power of money and leisure" to make the masses "the instruments of their own subjection."[38] In the campaign of 1844, he attended his first political meeting in twenty-five years, "and if anything could bring me on the stump," he declared vigorously, "it would be to help put down the bold and factious party that is now striving to place Mr. Clay in the chair of state." He denounced the Whig party as "much the falsest and most dangerous association

of the sort that has appeared in the country in my day."[39]

Yet Cooper's radicalism was soon to disappear. It was founded, we have seen, in the opposition of landed capital to business capital, the traditional dislike of the *rentier* for the speculator. But in the middle forties Cooper was suddenly asked to decide whether landed property was not in more peril from radicalism than from business. This question was raised sharply by the antirenters, a group of farmers seeking a revision of the semifeudal seigneurial relations between patroons and tenants in the huge estates along the Hudson. As a champion of the land, Cooper had rejoiced at the Jacksonian attacks on business; but now demagogues were extending the attack, under the same rallying cries, to the land itself. Would not their victory destroy the foundations of property the nation over? "The existence of true liberty among us, the perpetuity of the institutions, and the safety of public morals, are all dependent on putting down, wholly, absolutely, and unqualifiedly, the false and dishonest theories and statements that have been boldly advanced."[40] From a minor fault of democracy the "demagogue" was becoming a major threat, and the vicious agitators of the antirent trilogy showed Cooper's abhorrence of the class. The trilogy itself, emerging splendidly out of deeply felt and concrete emotions, demonstrated how profoundly Cooper's outlook was rooted in the existing land relationships. His obstinately personal attitude quickly changed any menace to these sacred arrangements into a national calamity.

The antirent troubles did more than shake his belief in popular rule. They

36 For the Jackson reference, *Home as Found,* 123.
37 Cooper to Bedford Brown, March 24, 1838, *loc. cit.*
38 Cooper, *The Redskins,* vi.

39 Cooper to C. A. Secor, *et al.,* September 8, 1844, *The Campaign,* September 21, 1844.
40 Cooper, *Satanstoe,* vii.

destroyed his Jeffersonian faith in the moral infallibility of life on the land. "We do not believe any more," he said, "in the superior innocence and virtue of a rural population."[41] His pessimism deepened. *The Lake Gun* (1850) set forth his fears for the Union, excited inevitably by demagogues; this time he clearly had Seward in mind. Despondency welled up most freely in his last work, *The Towns of Manhattan*. The book itself was destroyed by fire, but the introduction indicates the general temper. If property continued to be assailed, Cooper argued, it would take measures to protect itself. The result might well be fatal to popular liberties, but it would also be the just result of the abuse of popular liberties. There seemed but three possible solutions — military dictatorship, a return to original principles, or "the sway of money."[42] Of the three, the financial aristocracy seemed to him most likely. His old hatred of the commercial oligarchy had weakened, and he recognized it as the only bulwark of property. But his confidence in it was not strong, nor were his hopes for the future bright. This irresolute and baffled conclusion, all the more significant in a man of Cooper's ordinary certainty, suggests the depths of his despair. A year later he was dead.

4

The transcendentalists of Massachusetts constituted the one important literary group never much impressed by Jacksonian democracy. This immunity was all the more singular because for two occasional members, George Bancroft and Orestes A. Brownson, the relations between transcendentalism and democracy seemed close and vital. The Jack-sonians, in the minds of Bancroft and Brownson, were carrying on the same revolt against the dead hand of John Locke in politics which the transcendentalists were carrying on in religion. Both Democrat and transcendentalist agreed in asserting the rights of the free mind against the pretensions of precedents or institutions. Both shared a living faith in the integrity and perfectibility of man. Both proclaimed self-reliance. Both detested special groups claiming authority to mediate between the common man and the truth. Both aimed to plant the individual squarely on his instincts, responsible only to himself and to God. "The soul must and will assert its rightful ascendancy," exclaimed the *Bay State Democrat*, "over all those arbitrary and conventional forms which a false state of things has riveted upon society." "Democracy," cried Bancroft, "has given to conscience absolute liberty."[43]

But transcendentalism in its Concord form was infinitely individualistic, providing no means for reconciling the diverse intuitions of different men and deciding which was better and which worse. This did not worry most transcendentalists, who would allow Nicholas Biddle the authority of his inner voice and asked only to be allowed equally the authority of their own. The obligations of politics were not so flexible. Bancroft's great modification of transcendentalism was to add that the collective sense of the people provided the indispensable check on the anarchy of individual intuitions. "If reason is a universal faculty, the decision of the common mind is the nearest criterion of truth." Democracy thus perfected the insights

41 Cooper, *New York*, 56.
42 *New York*, 51.

43 *Bay State Democrat*, May 3, 1839; Bancroft, "Address to the Democratic Electors of Massachusetts," *Boston Post*, October 16, 1835.

of transcendentalism. "Individuals make proclamation of their own fancies; the spirit of God breathes through the combined intelligence of the people. . . . It is, when the multitude give council, that right purposes find safety; theirs is the fixedness that cannot be shaken; theirs is the understanding which exceeds in wisdom."[44]

For Bancroft and Brownson the battle against the past was indivisible, involving politics as much as philosophy. In his brilliant chapter on the Quakers in the second volume of his *History* (1837), Bancroft set forth in luminous prose his conception of the relations between the liberation of the soul of man and of his body. For Brownson conservatism in religion and in society were so nearly identical that he could observe of Victor Cousin, the French philosopher, "His works have made many young men among us Democrats." To Cousin himself he proudly declared, "We are combining philosophy with politics," adding that the Democratic party would soon adopt the views of the new school.[45] When Bancroft reviewed George Ripley's *Philosophical Miscellanies,* an anthology of French and German metaphysics, for the *Washington Globe,* he called it "a sort of manifesto of philosophical Democracy," and described how the glory of Jefferson had found new witnesses in the work of Cousin, Jouffroy and Constant.[46] An anonymous essayist in a Democratic paper even admonished the young men, in oddly Emersonian phrases, to "TRUST TO YOURSELF" and hymned the virtues of"*self-dependence.*"[47]

Yet, for all the inspiration some Democrats found in transcendentalism, the transcendentalists remained singularly unmoved by the exertions of the Democrats. From their book-lined studies or their shady walks in cool Concord woods, they found the hullabaloo of party politics unedifying and vulgar. The rebuke of Nature was crushing: "So hot? my little Sir." Life was short, and much better to contemplate verities and vibrate to that iron string than to make commitments to practicality. A political party, like society itself, was a joint-stock company, in which the members agreed, for the better securing of bread to each shareholder, to surrender the liberty and culture of the eater. "The virtue in most request is conformity. Self-reliance is its aversion."

But for the typical transcendentalist the flinching from politics perhaps expressed a failure they were seeking to erect into a virtue. The exigencies of responsibility were exhausting: much better to demand perfection and indignantly reject the half loaf, than wear out body and spirit in vain grapplings with overmastering reality. The headlong escape into perfection left responsibility far behind for a magic domain where mystic sentiment and gnomic utterance exorcised the rude intrusions of the world. But it was easier to rule the state from Concord than from Washington. And the state had to be ruled, it was the implacable vacuum: if Bronson Alcott preferred Fruitlands, he was not to complain when James K. Polk preferred the White House.

---

[44] Bancroft, "On the Progress of Civilization, or Reasons Why the Natural Association of Men of Letters Is with the Democracy," *Boston Quarterly Review,* I, 395 (October, 1838); Bancroft, "Address to the Democratic Electors of Massachusetts," *Boston Post,* October 16, 1835.

[45] Brownson to Bancroft, September 24, 1836, Bancroft Papers; Brownson to Cousin, June 23, 1838, Brownson Papers.

[46] *Washington Globe,* March 9, 1838.

[47] "To the Young Men," by "H. P.," *Bay State Democrat,* August 16, 1839.

Yet these were the worst, the pure transcendentalists, incapable of effective human relations, terrified of responsibility, given to transforming evasion into a moral triumph. The tougher-minded men on the transcendental margin recognized that certain obligations could not be shaken. The existence of society depended on a mutuality of confidence, the maintenance of which required that the demands of hunger, want and insecurity be met, lest desperation shatter the social chain. These basic agonies were not to be dissolved in the maternal embrace of the oversoul. George Ripley, unlike Bronson Alcott, did not despise those who held the ordinary affairs of life to be important. Whiggery in politics persuaded him as little as Whiggery in religion, and the energy of his friends Bancroft and Brownson stimulated him to work with transcendental insights on the ills of society. "He has fairly philosophized himself into Democracy," wrote Brownson in 1836. Ripley himself bravely declared to Bancroft a year later that "almost to a man, those who shew any marks of genius or intellectual enterprise are philosophical democrats." (The date was September 20, but he had no observations on the independent treasury.) The intellectual ferment of Boston was heady. "There is a great feeding on the mulberry leaves, and it will be hard if silken robes are not woven for the shining ones. . . . I almost hope to see the time, when religion, philosophy and politics will be united in a holy Trinity, for the redemption and blessedness of our social institutions."[48]

But Ripley's gestures toward the Democratic party were those of a pure young man engaged in audacious coquetry with an experienced woman of shady reputation. He smiled, inclined, almost yielded, then snatched away with an air of indignation, his head flushed with the pleasing excitement and his virtue intact. When Bancroft allowed some of Ripley's remarks to fill an anonymous paragraph in the *Boston Post*, Ripley wrote with alarm, "I insist on the distinction between the philosophical principles of democracy, and the democratic party in this country." (His timid advances were being taken with undue seriousness; almost he was invited to meet the family.) ". . . So it is with my young men. They have little faith in parties, but a great zeal for principles. They love nothing about the Whigs but the personal worth which they possess; but they are inclined to doubt whether the opponents of the Whigs are after all true democrats. It is certain, I must confess, that some of the warmest advocates of democratical principles, some who cherish the loftiest faith in the progress of humanity, are found in the Whig ranks."[49] The notes were revealing, for Ripley was not the most innocent of the transcendentalists. Yet he seemed to have no conception at all of, say, the role of measures and policies in underwriting "democratical principles." The diet of mulberry leaves might weave robes for the shining ones, but it gave small nourishment to a realistic view of society.

Ripley had escaped, but his conscience continued peremptory. Then, in 1840, a fairer and more chaste maiden appeared in the vision of Brook Farm, and he was saved from the worldly life of Politics. For him, and for the other transcendentalists who shared his inability to explain away suffering, Brook Farm ap-

[48] Brownson to Bancroft, September 24, 1836, Ripley to Bancroft, September 20, 1837, Bancroft Papers.

[49] Ripley to Bancroft, November 6, 1837, Bancroft Papers.

peared as a serious solution of the conditions which had driven Bancroft and Brownson into the arms of Party. Their faith was a variant of Utopianism, and Brook Farm appropriately ended up as a Fourierite phalanx.

5

The Oversoul thus comforted the tender transcendentalists, while the tough mowed the hay and raked the dirt at Brook Farm. But beyond the transcendentalists, accepting their inspiration but safe from their illusions, was Emerson, the wisest man of the day. He was too concretely aware of the complexities of experience to be altogether consoled by vagueness and reverie. The doctrine of compensation had its limits, and he was not received by Ripley's community. "At Education Farm, the noblest theory of life sat on the noblest figures of young men and maidens, quite powerless and melancholy. It would not rake or pitch a ton of hay; it would not rub down a horse; and the men and maidens it left pale and hungry."[50] Yet politics represent his greatest failure. He would not succumb to verbal panaceas, neither would he make the ultimate moral effort of Thoreau and cast off all obligation to society. Instead he lingered indecisively, accepting without enthusiasm certain relations to government but never confronting directly the implications of acceptance.

He acknowledged the claims of the Democratic party expounded so ardently by Bancroft and Brownson. "The philosopher, the poet, or the religious man, will, of course, wish to cast his vote with the democrat, for free-trade, for wide suffrage, for the abolition of legal cruelties in the penal code, and for facilitating

in every manner the access of the young and the poor to the sources of wealth and power."[51] He recognized, too, the inevitable drift of transcendentalism toward the democratic position. The first lecture of his series in 1839 on the "Present Age" was reported by Theodore Parker as "*Democratic-locofoco* throughout, and very much in the spirit of Brownson's article on Democracy and Reform in the last *Quarterly*." Bancroft left "in ecstasies . . . rapt beyond vision at the *locofocoism*," and one Boston conservative could only growl that Emerson must be angling for a place in the Custom House.[52]

Yet Emerson would go no farther. "Of the two great parties, which, at this hour, almost share the nation between them," he would lamely conclude, "I should say, that one has the best cause, and the other contains the best men."[53] This would have provided no excuse for inaction, even if it were true, for a man of Emersonian principle should follow his principle; but it was not even true.

Fear of institutions kept him cautious. A party seemed a form of church, and Emerson, a burnt child, shunned the fire. "Bancroft and Bryant," he said, "are historical democrats who are interested in dead or organized, but not in organizing, liberty."[54] He liked the *Washington Globe's* motto — "The world is governed too much" — though it appalled him that so many people read the paper. But in an imperfect world, should he not settle for "historical democrats" and *Washington Globes*, or at least remark on the alternative? Emerson was well aware of

[50] Emerson, *Essays* (World's Classics), 300.

[51] *Essays*, 407–408.
[52] Parker to Convers Francis, December 6, 1839, J. E. Cabot, *Memoir of Ralph Waldo Emerson*, 400–401.
[53] *Essays*, 407.
[54] *Journals*, VI, 315.

the discipline of choice. Yet here he failed himself, and ignored the responsibilities of his own moral position.

Fundamentally he did not care, and thus he was betrayed, almost without struggle, into the clichés of conservatism which had surrounded him from birth. In a flash of insight he could see that "banks and tariffs, the newspaper and caucus" were "flat and dull to dull people, but rest on the same foundations of wonder as the town of Troy, and the temple of Delphos."[55] Yet, in life at Concord, day in, day out, banks and tariffs were flat and dull to him. As he glanced at party contests, he was most impressed by "the meanness of our politics."[56]

He had little idea of the significance of the struggles of the eighteen-thirties. His ejaculation to Carlyle in 1834 — "a most unfit man in the Presidency has been doing the worst things" — about exhausted his conception of the Jackson administration.[57] His reluctance to break with the Whigs was increased by his invention of a statesman named Daniel Webster to whom he gave profound devotion and whom he carelessly confused with the popular Whig politician of the same name. "That great forehead which I followed about all my young days, from court-house to senate chamber, from caucus to street" cast a hypnotic spell over a man otherwise hard to fool.[58] His comments, scattered over two decades of loyalty, show a literary fascination with the massiveness of personality, the stately rhetoric, the marble brow and face black as thunder; but little concern

for his views on practical policy. This Webster was a mirage peculiar to Emerson. For Bryant, Bancroft, Cooper, Whitman and Hawthorne, Webster was the most vulnerable celebrity of the day.[59] But for Emerson he remained a great statesman — until Webster finally ran up against an issue which really excited Emerson's imagination and commanded his full attention, and the speech on the Compromise of 1850 disclosed to Emerson what he should have known for years. The steady wisdom of the sage of Concord faltered, in this one field, into sentimentality.

6

Of all the New England group who shunned political choice, Thoreau alone lived at a degree of moral tension which imposed responsibilities equivalent to those borne by men who sought to govern. He could not delude himself with fantasies of easy salvation, like Alcott or Ripley, nor could he accept the status of citizenship, like Emerson, and dally with its obligations. For him the moral life admitted but one possibility: the complete assumption of all responsi-

---

[55] *Essays*, 285.

[56] *Essays*, 185.

[57] Emerson to Carlyle, May 14, 1834, *Correspondence of Thomas Carlyle and Ralph Waldo Emerson, 1843–1872*, C. E. Norton, ed., I, 16.

[58] Emerson to Carlyle, August 8, 1839, *ibid.*, I, 255.

[59] Webster was the butt of the Democratic literary men, as his peculiar combination of cynicism and external moral grandeur made inevitable. Hawthorne's sketch of Webster as "Old Stony Phiz" in "The Great Stone Face" is well known and penetrating, presenting him as "a man of mighty faculties and little aims, whose life, with all its high performances, was vague and empty, because no high purpose had endowed it with reality." Hawthorne, *Writings*, III, 51. For Bancroft's ribald running comment on Webster, see his correspondence with Van Buren. Bryant's famous editorial on Webster's humor in the *New York Evening Post* of November 20, 1837, is to be found in Bryant, *Prose Writings*, Parke Godwin, ed., II, 383–385. A typical Cooper reference is in *The Monikins*, 414. Whitman summed them all up with his brief remark that Webster was "overrated more than any other public man ever prominent in America." *Brooklyn Eagle*, April 11, 1846, *Gathering of the Forces*, II, 182.

bility by the individual. The highest
good, said Thoreau, was the living
unity of the ethical consciousness and its
direct, solid expression in art and life.

In practice he achieved the goal best
by a deliberate reduction of life to its
essentials — a cabin by blue Walden,
blackberries in the summer, the indomi-
table woodchuck, the wild sweet song of
the evening robin, the geese flying low
over the woods, the last blaze of sun in
the west. But he could not dwell forever
at Walden; he had other lives to live;
and he returned to society, now fulfilling
his singleness of feeling by fusing his superb style till the words, as he said, fell
like boulders across the page. Back in
the world again, he was face to face with
the enemies of the moral life: the new
industrialism, which would deform the
moral self, and the state, which would
corrupt it. In society people lived in
quiet desperation, sick at heart, their
integrity menaced, clouded and compromised. The only man worth having,
thought Thoreau, was the man of principle, and he was worth any expense to
the state.

The state, he said, had no moral status.
Its rule was expediency, its method,
force. It had no right to act on its subjects in terms of obligation and duty.
Individuals could have no moral relation
to it: the soul was indefeasible, and its
burdens could not be assumed by the
state. Men should tolerate the state in
its milder moments, but, when it seeks
to violate their integrity by immoral actions of its own, they must shake themselves free of all complicity. "The only
government that I recognize — and it
matters not how few are at the head of
it, or how small its army — is that power
that establishes justice in the land, never
that which establishes injustice." Was
not the presumption always against the
state, that "semihuman tiger or ox, stalking over the earth, with its heart taken
out and the top of its brain shot away"?
"Is it not possible," he cried, "that an
individual may be right and a government wrong?" Man must achieve his
moral unity, if necessary at the cost of
civil disobedience. This was the sublim-
est heroism "for once we are lifted out
of the trivialness and dust of politics into
the region of truth and manhood." Only
a succession of *men,* carrying out such
defiances, could tame the semihuman
tiger till the state should recognize the
individual "as a higher and independent
power, from which all its own power and
authority are derived, and treats him
accordingly."[60]

Thoreau's case was consistent and ir-
revocable. It was his by bitter conquest,
and into holding it he poured the energies of his life. No position could be
more exhausting and more pitiless. The
relentless pressure of everlasting responsibility beat down on the frail individual,
deprived of the possibility of diffusing
his guilt among society, alone against the
universe, armed only with his own inner
righteousness.

Few men could stand the unimaginable strain: for most it leads to hypocrisy
or collapse. "Man is neither angel nor
brute," observed Pascal, "and the unfortunate thing is that he who would act the
angel acts the brute." It is for this reason
that society has proscribed those evaders
who claim the prerogatives of a Thoreau
without undergoing his intense moral
ordeal. Civil disobedience is justified
only by the sternest private obedience,
and angels are all too likely to turn into
brutes. Thoreau earned his beliefs and
his immunities. Little men, covering

---

[60] Thoreau, "Plea for Captain John Brown,"
Works, IV, 430, 429, 437; "Civil Disobedience,"
Works, IV, 387.

cowardice with a veil of self-righteousness, lay claim to the exemptions of a Thoreau with the most intolerable pretense. The camp followers of a war which he fought, they are presently the camp followers of a war fought by the rest of society, accepting the protection of the state but disclaiming any obligations. Their performance should not compromise his case. The writings and life of Thoreau presented democracy with a profound moral challenge.

7

Thoreau said Nay to the claims of democracy, but Walt Whitman sent back the thunderous affirmation, echoing off the roof-tops of the world. Twenty-one in the year of Tippecanoe, Whitman was already up to his neck in radical Democratic politics. In a year, he would be speaking at a huge party mass meeting and contributing to the *Democratic Review.* In 1844 he would join the movement to draft Silas Wright for Governor and elect James K. Polk. In 1846 he would become editor of the *Brooklyn Daily Eagle,* and while in Brooklyn serve on the Democratic General Committee and the Fourth of July Celebration Committee.

Brooklyn knew him as Walter Whitman, an amiable and relaxed young man, with a ruddy pleasant face and a short beard, wandering indolently through the bustling streets with an easy word for everyone, from merchant to cartman. After his stint for the *Eagle* he would go down to Gray's Swimming Bath at the foot of Fulton Street and lounge for twenty minutes in the water. Then the office boy would give him a shower, and he would take the evening ferry back to New York through the dying sunset.[61]

[61] Whitman, *Gathering of the Forces,* I, xix–xxiii.

("Flood-tide below me! I see you face to face! Clouds of the west — sun there half an hour high — I see you also face to face.")

These were days of quiet immersion in the flood of experience which would later sweep aside the conventions of verse to achieve their own expression, poignant, tender, gusty, barbaric, incoherent and magnificent. He drank in not just the sea gulls, floating high in the air on motionless wings, their bodies lit up glistening yellow by the setting sun, not just the men and women on the street, "the blab of the pave, tires of carts, sluff of boot-soles, talk of the promenaders." He drank in the feelings of the people themselves, their anxieties, hopes, aspirations.

For Whitman none of the doubts of Thoreau. For him only a vigorous acceptance and mastery of the democratic opportunity. "To attack the turbulence and destructiveness of the Democratic spirit," he said, "is an old story. . . . Why, all that is good and grand in any political organization in the world, is the result of this turbulence and destructiveness; and controlled by the intelligence and common sense of such a people as the Americans, it never has brought harm, and never can."

Politics a noisy show, unworthy of the attention of serious men? "It is the fashion of a certain set to assume to despise 'politics' . . . they look at the fierce struggle, and at the battle of principles and candidates, and their weak nerves retreat dismayed from the neighborhood of such scenes of convulsion. But to our view, the spectacle is always a grand one — full of the most august and sublime attributes."

The enthusiasm of democracy an evil? "All the noisy tempestuous scenes of politics witnessed in this country — all the excitement and strife, even — are *good* to behold. They evince that the *people act;* they are the discipline of the young giant, getting his maturer strength."

Is democracy then perfect? Let no one be distracted by detail. "We know, well enough, that the workings of Democracy are not always justifiable, in every trivial point. But the great winds that purify the air, without which nature would flag into ruin — are they to be condemned because a tree is prostrated here and there, in their course?"[62]

Through the blast of Whitman's prose sounded the answer to Thoreau. Man, he affirmed, could have a relation of moral significance to the state, so long as the state was truly the expression of the popular will and the best in man. Perfection? No, for the state, like the people which created it, had failings and flaws. (Whitman, unlike Thoreau, had a certain sympathy for imperfections.) Belief in the people should not be discouraged by trivialities or weakened by petty disappointments. In the greatness of his faith in the people Whitman could not but declare his faith in the possibilities of democratic government.

In 1856 Henry Thoreau and Walt Whitman, meeting for the first time, had a stiff conversation in Whitman's attic study in New York. Thoreau felt that he did not get very far. "Among the few things which I chanced to say, I remember that one was . . . that I did not think much of America or of politics, and so on, which may have been somewhat of a damper to him." No doubt it was, and Whitman carried away a vivid impression of Thoreau's "disdain for men (for Tom, Dick, and Harry): inability to appreciate the average life — even the

exceptional life: it seemed to me a want of imagination. He couldn't put his life into any other life — realize why one man was so and another was not so: was impatient with other people on the street and so forth." They had, as Whitman recalled it, rather a hot discussion. "It was a bitter difference: it was rather a surprise to me to meet in Thoreau such a very aggravated case of superciliousness."[63]

Thoreau himself contemplated no social reconstruction. He simply wanted to live his own life under standards higher than men like Whitman, who could put off some of their own guilt on the rest of society. But the mass of men must live in society, or in their visions of a new society; and while there is room for superciliousness in a democracy, it provides an inadequate basis for a political philosophy. The impulse of Whitman was healthier for the social state. His life was spent in an exultation in the potentialities, and a scourging of the failures, of democracy. If the state was not to be a semihuman tiger, with its heart taken out and the top of its brain shot away, it would probably be due more to the Whitmans than to the Thoreaus. As Whitman himself declared, "There is no week nor day nor hour when tyranny may not enter upon this country, if the people lose their supreme confidence in themselves, — and lose their roughness and spirit of defiance — Tyranny may always enter — there is no charm no bar against it — the only bar against it is a large resolute breed of men."[64]

---

[62] Whitman, "American Democracy," *Brooklyn Eagle*, April 20, 1847, *Gathering of the Forces*, I, 3–6.

[63] Thoreau to Harrison Blake, December 7, 1856, *Works*, XI, 347; Traubel, *With Whitman in Camden*, I, 212. See also H. S. Canby, *Thoreau*, 412–417.

[64] "Notes for Lectures on Democracy and 'Adhesiveness,' " C. J. Furness, *Walt Whitman's Workshop*, 58.

Ralph Henry Gabriel: EMERSON AND THOREAU

Ralph Henry Gabriel, formerly professor of history at Yale, was also general editor of the series of volumes entitled Pageant of America. *In this chapter from his book* The Course of American Democratic Thought, *he gives us a distinctly different view of what Schlesinger called "the typical transcendentalist." To Gabriel that term would be a misnomer, for certainly one trait characterizing the transcendentalists is their emphasis upon the uniqueness of every individual. This does not, however, really lead them to an avoidance of social and political issues. Some, as Schlesinger notes, did actively participate in politics. But is it correct to say as he also does that others "like Emerson and Thoreau . . . spent years quietly ignoring politics"? Gabriel, who places great emphasis upon the influence of the frontier, sees Emerson and Thoreau as adopting an alternative means to social reform, that of personal example and of exhortation. They were, he thinks, attempting to adapt the individualism of the frontier, which in many ways was an expression of the desire to escape from the trammels of society, to "an era in which society was closing in upon the individual." In so doing, "they served as spokesmen for an emerging democratic faith," and were thus, in their own fashion, helping to carry out the Jacksonian program.*

IN the middle period of the nineteenth century the village of Concord in the Commonwealth of Massachusetts stirred with new life. Here Hawthorne wrote polished studies of damaged souls; here Bronson Alcott turned from schoolmastering to philosophy. Here Emerson, during summer days, walked often along the town's main street past stores where farmers' families came to trade, and continued on the thoroughfare after it had become a dusty country road winding into the surrounding hills. At the northern edge of the village, the Concord River was crossed by a bridge where in 1775 the opening battle of the Revolution had been fought. The patriots of Concord proudly recalled that first blow struck for American liberty by Concord men.

Their bridge was becoming a shrine to which pilgrims came to venerate the spot where Americans first died for the ideal of constitutional democracy. In 1837 Concord erected a battle monument beside the bridge. Concord, therefore, was no ordinary village metropolis of a rural area. It had a past. It was old — several times as old as contemporary villages of equal size in the Upper Mississippi Valley. Many of its houses were, according to American standards, venerable. The mood of Puritanism, which had dominated its thought in the seventeenth century, still clung to it like wisps of fog that the morning sun has not yet driven from the fields. In its periodic town meetings its quiet life was governed by the methods of a well-tried democracy.

To these gatherings went Emerson, to discuss with his neighbors the problems of highway upkeep and the management of the Common.

Citizen Emerson was one of the atoms that made up the Concord community. So was his young friend, Henry Thoreau, who, by the 1850's, had acquired a reputation for being a little queer. There was mild neighborhood curiosity in 1845 concerning his lonely sojourn in a hut at Walden Pond not far away. In 1848 the villagers of Concord sometimes saw Thoreau working in Emerson's garden when the latter was in Europe. After the philosopher's return, the townspeople often watched the older and the younger man stride off together on a hike across the neighboring fields. There was some shaking of heads on the part of the church-goers. The proper business of a man, according to Puritan ethics, was work. To spend a week day alone or with a friend, as both Emerson and Thoreau frequently did, loitering about Walden Pond without even the excuse of hunting or fishing, was little short of a sin. To the scandal of the neighborhood, moreover, Thoreau refused to attend religious worship; Emerson, who had quit the ministry for what seemed to be no good cause, was only a little better. Emerson, however, was easily forgiven. He was a true son of Concord who, on the Fourth of July, 1837, had disposed of the pretensions of the rival patriots of Lexington when he had read his "Concord Hymn" beside the new battle monument:

By the rude bridge that arched the flood,
  Their flag to April's breeze unfurled,
Here once the embattled farmers stood
  And fired the shot heard round the world.

Concord in the Middle Period was the scene of another battle. Like the tiff of April 19, 1775, this was also a fight for liberty. There were no shock troops engaged, however, for Emerson believed neither in numbers nor in disciples. He put his faith in battalions of one or two. Only such minorities, he thought, could accomplish concrete social advances. In Concord in the 1840's and 1850's, Emerson and Thoreau marched out, like the minute men of old, to fight for new ideals. The older man was not the originator of the democratic faith, for that cluster of social beliefs rose spontaneously among the Americans of his generation, but he was its greatest prophet. Emerson sensed the individualism of his rural America. He believed in it wholeheartedly, yet he felt that the emerging faith of democracy, in spite of its momentary victories, was imprisoned within a militant and advancing evangelical Christianity. Protestantism, he thought, was a lost cause. The problem of the hour for him was the rescue, from entangling Christian superstitions, of the great doctrines of the fundamental law, of progress, and of the free individual. When Harvard, his Alma Mater, refused to let him again speak to the student body after his address in 1838 to the Divinity School, he anticipated no quarter from his theological adversaries. As for Thoreau, he thought conventional Christianity little better than the medicine bundle carried by the Indian brave for protection.

In his later years Emerson, become famous, put shutters outside the lower half of his study windows to protect himself from the world. But in the two decades before the Civil War he traveled on lecture tours for thousands of miles in the crowded promiscuity of river steamboats and railroad trains. He knew the *genus Americanus* from first-hand contact. Emerson, like the commercial drummer, made his living by traveling, and the Concord philosopher was extraordinarily successful in vending his intellectual wares. His success creates a problem for the historian.

Emerson, who lectured quietly on the lyceum platform, was the antithesis of that familiar American type, the camp-meeting evangelist. No contrast could be more complete than that between the serenity of the scholar from Concord and the excited emotionalism of the exhorter. Nor was the difference limited to manner. Emerson's lectures were full of subtleties; their intellectual level was high; they usually contained passages which were over the heads of audiences untrained in philosophical thinking. By contrast, the preachers of evangelical Protestantism dispensed a simple theology. They did not normally tax the minds of their hearers; the clergy appealed from the head to the heart. The phenomenon of Emerson, ex-Unitarian minister from New England, making a success of lecturing in the trans-Appalachian stronghold of evangelical Protestantism in the middle decades of the nineteenth century is one of the more significant episodes of the age.

Emerson's success was not due to his preaching of a mystical, pantheistic transcendentalism. He talked to practical men for most of whom mysticism was, in all probability, incomprehensible. That particular type of religious experience has never been important in American culture. Emerson impressed the common folk of his generation because he preached a philosophy of individualism that not only seemed to set men free, but to provide them with dynamic, creative energy. He gave the doctrine of the free individual sharpness of definition, causing it to emerge, with the clarity of an etching, from the cloudy background of half-formulated ideas.

Throughout his early years Emerson struggled almost constantly with problems raised by the varieties of Christianity which were prevalent in the United States of his day. He never went through a Calvinist stage, so he did not have to formulate an answer to the problem of how to reconcile democracy's trust in the common man with Calvin's doctrine of the complete corruptness of human nature. Nor was Emerson compelled to undertake to harmonize Calvinistic determinism with the idea that in a democracy free men create and rule the government under which they live. For the early Emerson, Protestantism meant Unitarianism; one of the familiar stories in American history is the narrative of Emerson's growing discontent with the "pale negations" of this system, and his final decision to abandon the security of a comfortable pastorate for the hazards of independent lecturing and writing. Unitarianism, in Emerson's opinion, did not provide the dynamics which are necessary for individual creation. Unitarianism freed men from old superstitions but, when these had been thrown off, its power was spent.

Emerson, traveling over America, was aware of the forces released by evangelical Protestantism. He knew the power of that experience called conversion. He understood the evangelical concept of the free individual. But he had no use for the theology which lay behind the conversion, for it rested upon the authority of a literally inspired Scripture. For Emerson the Bible was no more inspired than some other great books. At best it recorded the experience with living of other men in other days. The poet-philosopher was willing to learn from the past, but he sought final sanctions in his own experience in the present. Man, thought Emerson, is a creature of nature.

From nature he derives his individuality and his freedom. He must find in nature, rather than in the Bible, that ultimate authority which makes his freedom possible.

To Emerson the popular American version of the doctrine of the free individual was the beginning, rather than the end, of social philosophy. In American communities of the period, individualism meant the independence of the shopkeeper or of the husbandman, each man managing his affairs according to his lights and his tastes. Popular individualism emphasized social atoms; the one closely knit group which was universally recognized and approved was the family. To Emerson a man appeared to be part of something; Emerson's taste was for wholes rather than for parts. He rejected atomism, whether it appeared in social or in scientific thought. As an undergraduate at Harvard, he had studied natural philosophy only to find the scientists preoccupied with the parts of nature. Following the path of scientists since the days of Galileo and Newton, they broke down matter into molecules and molecules into atoms. But Emerson basically had as little sympathy for test tube seers as for crystal gazers. The philosophies of both were, in his opinion, destined to come to a bad end. The curse of science was its sole dependence upon the intellect. "Pure intellect," remarked Emerson, paying his respects to the eighteenth century Enlightenment, "is the pure devil when you have got off all the masks of Mephistopheles."[1] Reason, he observed, when men depend solely upon it, leads only to science. Feeling, to him, was as important as intellectual analyses in the apprehensions of nature, and, significant though science is, nature can teach man more than Newton's materialism. Scientific naturalism in Emerson's day emphasized the parts, the atoms which were thought to be the ultimate units of matter. It pictured the universe as a vast cosmic machine whose wheels within wheels fitted and worked together with infinite nicety. The incompleteness of the atom and of the individual man left Emerson dissatisfied; it outraged his aesthetic sense as did a musical discord. "To a sound judgment," he remarked, "the most abstract truth is the most practical."[2] He put behind him all systems which emphasized the many; he turned his thought — and his feelings — to the discovery of a philosophy of the one. By so doing he set his face against the prevailing winds of social and scientific thought in nineteenth century America. "Whoso would be a man must be a nonconformist,"[3] he explained quietly as he bested his way forward.

"We walked this afternoon to Edmund Hosmer's and Walden Pond," Emerson recorded in his journal on April 9, 1842. "The south wind blew and filled with bland and warm light the dry and sunny woods. The last year's leaves blew like birds through the air. As I sat on the bank of the Drop, or God's Pond, and saw the amplitude of the little water, what space, what verge, the little scudding fleets of ripples found to scatter and spread from side to side and take so much time to cross the pond, and saw how the water seemed made for the wind and the wind for the water, dear playfellows for each other, — I said to my companion, I declare this world is so beautiful that I can hardly believe it

[1] Bliss Perry, *Heart of Emerson's Journals*, 207.

[2] R. W. Emerson, "Nature," *Emerson's Complete Works* (Riverside ed., 1883), I, 10.

[3] R. W. Emerson, "Self-Reliance," *Complete Works* (Riverside ed., 1883), II, 51.

exists."[4] Emerson did not see nature in one of its grander aspects as he walked that afternoon beside Walden Pond. Men stand in awe on the rim of the canyon of the Colorado or beneath El Capitan towering above the Merced. Emerson saw only a simple New England landscape, a commonplace composition which included water, a strip of sand and rocks, and the encircling woods. Any scientist could analyze it into its component parts. The farmers who tilled the fields lying on the flanks of the hills could do that and more. They knew where the muskrats built their tunnels and where, in the autumn, the farm dog was likely to tree a raccoon. The lore of the particular had no interest for Emerson that day at Walden. The aspect of the scene which impressed him was that "the water seemed made for the wind and the wind for the water." And the feeling came to him that he, an individual man, was made for both and both were made for him. The essence of the scene was the unity which bound the parts together and which fused the observer with the observed. In such fusion Emerson experienced the exaltation of a mystic. "The world is so beautiful," he said half in pain, "that I can hardly believe it exists." He made this unity his god. "We see the world by piece," he remarked at another time, "as the sun, the moon, the animal, the tree; but the whole, of which these are the shining parts, is the soul."[5] Emerson came to an understanding of the nature and power of that vast impersonal spirit, that Over-Soul, which is the ultimate reality of nature. "Standing on the bare ground, — my head bathed in the blithe air, and uplifted into infinite space, — all mean egotism vanishes. I

become a transparent eyeball; I am nothing; I see all; the currents of the Universal Being circulate through me; I am part or parcel of God."[6]

So Emerson penetrated, as he thought, the material husks of reality to its core. Looking out from here, as from the center of a sphere, the poet saw nature and man taking on new meanings. Nature "is a great shadow pointing always to the sun behind us." A man laboring for a brief day on the earth strives for food to eat and for protection against the elements. He has the body and some of the ways of an animal. He is a transient phenomenon important today, forgotten tomorrow. His petty, untutored egotism, like that of some self-important ant, causes him to listen wistfully to the preacher who asserts that man will live forever — in another world. What a picture, thought Emerson — the Christian preacher trying with a bellows of egotism to fan into flame that divine spark, the human soul. What is man? He is a conduit through which flows moral energy, the very essence of the Over-Soul. He is a part of God; his body is an instrument to work out the purposes of God. "Within man is the soul of the whole; the wise silence; the universal beauty, to which every part and particle is equally related; the eternal One."[7] And what of eternity? Emerson knew eternity that day at Walden Pond, when the breeze disturbed the leaves of other summers, for eternity is the realization of the unity between the transient individual and the everlasting One.

In this concept of the individual and of his relation to God may be found the key to Emerson's social philosophy. Society, he thought, is an aggregation of

4 Perry, 152.
5 R. W. Emerson, "Over-Soul," Complete Works, II, 253.

6 R. W. Emerson, "Nature," op. cit., I, 15–16.
7 R. W. Emerson, "Over-Soul," op. cit., II, 253.

cohering individuals. The centrifugal forces tending to disrupt it are all too evident. They were clear enough in Emerson's day when section was muttering against section, and when the rich mill owner was too often ruthlessly exploiting the wage earner, his wife, and his child. The poor men of the East and of the West were asserting the power of their mass strength and, putting Andrew Jackson in the presidency, were smashing that symbol of financial autocracy, the great bank of the United States. Why did not democratic America, filled with greed and strife, collapse into futile chaos? Because within and behind all men was the eternal, stabilizing, unifying Over-Soul, God. The stresses in American society might seem alarming to little minds devoid of faith. They would not, however, prove fatal. Emerson welcomed even an increase of American heterogeneity. Let the immigrants come. "The energy of Irish, Germans, Swedes, Poles, and Cossacks, and all the European tribes, — and of the Africans, and of the Polynesians, — will construct a new race, a new religion, a new state, a new literature, which will be as vigorous as the new Europe which came out of the smelting-pot of the Dark Ages. . . ."[8] Here was a robust optimism born of faith.

Emerson had, however, few illusions concerning the breed of American politicians, local or national. He once remarked that, if he were ever in danger of loving life unduly, he would attend a caucus of the followers of Andrew Jackson, and "I doubt not the unmixed malignity, the withering selfishness, the impudent vulgarity, that mark those meetings would speedily cure me of my appetite

for longevity."[9] Yet his faith was invincible. Within each of these slattern democrats was the spirit of the One. The mechanic plying his trade or the farmer breaking the prairie held in his hand, if he could only be made to understand it, the hammer of Thor. One such Kansas husbandman, born of the common herd, sensed his power. He struck one blow for righteousness; America quaked from Cape Cod to the Rockies. Then John Brown of Osawatomie made "the gallows glorious like the cross."

To Emerson, Brown was merely another proof of the power and importance of the free individual. The philosopher himself was such a minority of one. He sought no disciples; he formed no cult. Emerson emphasized to enthusiastic admirers that no man could follow him step by step and be a disciple. All men are different; each expresses in his own peculiar way the Over-Soul within him. To attempt to superimpose upon dissimilar men an intellectual stereotype or a fixed pattern of action was for Emerson the unforgivable sin. Regimentation, he thought, destroyed the souls of men.

When Emerson was preparing the lectures published as *Essays, First Series,* the collectivist philosophy of Charles Fourier was much discussed in America. Albert Brisbane and Horace Greeley were its New-World prophets. The decade of the 1840's was a time of ferment as America slowly recovered from the depression of 1837–1842. American mores were not fixed; the desire for experiment was in the air. The famous Brook Farm Community near Concord did not at first accept the Fourierist pattern, but tried out the collectivist ideas of the Concord transcendentalists. Emerson's attitude toward the Brook Farm venture illus-

[8] Quoted by Stuart P. Sherman in *Essays and Poems of Emerson with an Introduction by Stuart P. Sherman,* 1921, xxxiv.

[9] *Ibid.,* xxxii.

trates the quality of his thought. He, the philosopher of individualism, did not dismiss collectivism with sarcasm. He attended the preliminary conferences which created the Farm. Here was a social experiment to be honestly undertaken. It might demonstrate that collectivism is the handmaid of individualism; it might prove that the soul of the individual man can develop more readily and express itself more freely in a communal than in a competitive social pattern. Emerson listened to the plans of the eager founders. On October 17, 1840, he set down his conclusions in his *Journal.* "Yesterday George and Sophia Ripley, Margaret Fuller and Alcott discussed here the Social Plans [Brook Farm]. I wished to be convinced, to be thawed, to be made nobly mad by the kindling before my eye of a new dawn of human piety. But this scheme was arithmetic and comfort; this was a hint borrowed from Tremont House and the United States Hotel; a rage in our poverty and politics to live rich and gentlemanlike, an anchor to leeward against a change of weather; a prudent forecast on the probable issue of the great questions of Pauperism and Poverty. And not once could I be inflamed, but sat aloof and thoughtless; my voice faltered and fell. It was not the cave of persecution which is the palace of spiritual power, but only a room in the Astor House hired for the Transcendentalists. I do not wish to remove from my present prison to a prison a little larger. I wish to break all prisons. I have not yet conquered my own house. It irks me and repents me. Shall I raise the siege of this hencoop, and march baffled away to a pretended siege of Babylon? It seems to me that so to do were to dodge the problem I am set to solve, and to hide my impotency in the thick of a crowd. I can see too,

afar, — that I should not find myself more than now, — no, not so much, in that select, but not by me selected, fraternity. Moreover, to join this body would be to traverse all my long-trumpeted theory, and the instinct which spoke from it, that one man is a counterpoise to a city, — that a man is stronger than a city, that his solitude is more prevalent and beneficent than the concert of crowds."[10]

So Emerson rejected the experimental collectivism of his day. It is the individual man in whose heart the Over-Soul, the Universal Mind, finds a dwelling place who is all important, Emerson concluded, in spite of Brook Farm. Standing on the frontier between the past, with its social heritage, and the future, with its promises, he fashions his own history and with it that of nations and of the world. Too long the dogmas of an outworn Christianity have kept man from understanding the power that lies within him. In the United States where the democratic faith provides the ideals by which to measure conduct, men are beginning to discover the individual, but their vision of what constitutes a man is blurred by old theologies. Teach these sons to know themselves and the nation will be on the march toward an empire of the spirit. Such an America, rising on the western shore of the Atlantic, must become a flaming beacon, lighting for all the world the path of human destiny.

"I spoke of friendship," wrote Emerson in his *Journal* in 1848, "but my friends and I are fishes in our habit. As for taking Thoreau's arm, I should as soon take the arm of an elm tree."[11] "Henry is military," he added five years later. "He seems stubborn and implacable, al-

10 Bliss Perry, *Heart of Emerson's Journals,* 156–157.
11 *Ibid.,* 238.

ways manly and wise, but rarely sweet. One would say that, as Webster could never speak without an antagonist, so Henry does not feel himself except in opposition. He wants a fallacy to expose, a blunder to pillory, requires a little sense of victory, a roll of the drums, to call his powers into full exercise."[12] Emerson was, perhaps, a bit unfair to his young friend, who had been a member of his household, and who, after some schoolmastering and a little surveying, was in 1845 retiring from society to his hut on Walden Pond. *Walden,* which Thoreau distilled from that experiment, was more affirmation than rejection. Even so, to the end of his days the celibate pencil-maker remained an adversary of American civilization, a stiff-backed solitary soldier who tramped stubbornly in the opposite direction from the army's line of march.

Thoreau's New England was bustling with industrial enterprise. The Holyoke dam first successfully held back the Connecticut in 1849, the year in which Thoreau published *Civil Disobedience.* Almost every New England stream was turning the wheels of some mill or factory. Boston was the rendezvous of entrepreneurs great and small, men skilled in the stratagems and tactics, the deceptive retreats and surprise attacks essential to the art of pecuniary competition. Thoreau was shocked at the thought of a man spending his years at such an occupation when nature had given so short a time to live. In 1843 he read with growing anger in an English pamphlet of that economy of plenty which would result from the harnessing of the powers of nature and making them serve men through machines. "Fellowmen!" exclaimed the enthusiastic innovator, J. A.

Etzler, "I promise to show the means of creating a paradise within ten years, where everything desirable for human life may be had by every man in superabundance, without labor, and without pay."[13] For Thoreau machines were gadgets which made life so complicated that they made living difficult; they were burdens which men carried on their backs; they blighted alike the lives of the children who tended them in factories and of the entrepreneurs who had them built. Thoreau never compromised with the machine; he never ceased to despise — and to pity — those men whose days were filled with business and whose goal was wealth. Fortunes, like machines, increased the difficulty of living. Thoreau lived for many months in his hut at Walden to prove to himself and to whosoever might be interested that nature is sufficient, that the machine confines rather than frees the spirit. The machine, he thought, was becoming a menace to the free individual.

But a more serious danger, at the moment, was, in his opinion, the State. When he found the State dominated by the crude materialism of a rising industrialism, he withdrew and refused to pay his poll tax. His opposition to the body politic became embittered when the federal government called for soldiers for the war against Mexico in the years from 1846 to 1848. *Civil Disobedience,* written when Thoreau was thirty-two, is the best American expression of the philosophy that the State is potentially or actually a malevolent institution, a threat to the liberty of the individual, and, being such an agency whose powers must be reduced to a minimum. Such an attitude had led to the writing of bills of rights into state constitutions during the Revo-

---

[12] *Ibid.,* 263.

[13] Henry David Thoreau, *Writings of Thoreau* (New Riverside ed., 1893), X, 38.

lution and to the addition of the first ten amendments to the Constitution of 1787.

Thoreau's argument assumed that the individual comes into the world to live and not necessarily to make it better. This particular and separate personality has a conscience enabling him to know, and directing him to obey, the "higher law" of his nature. The citizen must not "resign his conscience to the legislator." He cannot accept the principle of majority rule; "any man more right than his neighbors constitutes a majority of one already." Majorities, in deciding what is expedient, rule by force. They make the law; the State is their instrument for its enforcement. "Laws never made a man a whit more just." The men who serve the government too often forget conscience and obey force; the State robs them of their manhood. "Visit the Navy-yard," said Thoreau, "and behold a marine, such a man as an American government can make, or such as it can make a man with its black arts, — a mere shadow and reminiscence of humanity, a man laid out alive and standing, and already, as one may say, buried under arms." To Thoreau the professional soldier personified the negation of individual freedom.

If, perchance, the State be just, added the militant Thoreau, let the citizen share in its virtue. But if it be unjust, and such is the common characteristic of government, let him remember that "all men recognize the right of revolution; that is, the right to refuse allegiance to, and to resist the government, when its tyranny or its inefficiency are great and unendurable." Thoreau made no distinction between federal and local power; because Massachusetts did not refuse completely to co-operate in the war of spoliation against Mexico, he called her "a drab of state, a cloth-o'-silver slut." And it was a Massachusetts tax which he refused to pay. He advocated and practiced passive resistance.

Before his mind rose a vision of a better world, not the Paradise of the Christians, nor the communal utopia of the Fourierists, but one dominated by the individual, free in all things save in the right to violate his conscience. "There will never be a really free and enlightened State until the State comes to recognize the individual as a higher and independent power, from which all its own power and authority are derived, and treats him accordingly. I please myself with imagining a State at last which can afford to be just to all men, and to treat the individual with respect as a neighbor; which even would not think it inconsistent with its own repose if a few were to live aloof from it, not meddling with it, nor embraced by it, who fulfilled all the duties of neighbors and fellow-men. A State which bore this kind of fruit, and suffered it to drop off as fast as it ripened, would prepare the way for a still more perfect and glorious State, which also I have imagined, but not yet anywhere seen."[14] Disclaim it though he did, Thoreau was a crusader for a better world.

Thoreau was less interested in Protestantism than was Emerson, the ex-minister. The younger man dismissed Christianity as a spent force and, therefore a factor to be ignored. More than Emerson, Thoreau directed his thought toward the future. He saw, not always clearly, but with better vision than any of his contemporaries, new forces arising to threaten the great doctrines of the moral law and of the free individual. One of these was industrialism, and another was nationalism which enhanced the power

[14] See foregoing quotations from "Civil Disobedience," *Writings of Thoreau* (New Riverside ed., 1893), Vol. X.

of the State. Had Thoreau not been stricken down in middle life, he would have lived to see the democratic faith bent to the service of the great industrialist and used to defend the economic overlord against majorities of weaker men seeking to put limits upon irresponsible and autocratic power. Thoreau, however, scented danger afar. He tried to establish, before it was too late, the conclusion that a philosophy of materialism is a formula of death. As for the second menace, the rising power of the State, Thoreau, happily, did not live to hear from across the ocean in the post-Versailles twentieth century the rhythm of the tramping feet of millions of men, of youths, and even of little children, or to see Christianity supplanted by State worship.

Emerson was often puzzled by the words and the doings of his brilliant friend. In spite of their mutual sympathy and of their common transcendentalism, they were, in some respects, far apart. The older man shook his head over the Walden experiment. "Henry Thoreau," he remarked, "is like the wood-god who solicits the wandering poet and draws him into antres vast and deserts idle, and bereaves him of his memory, and leaves him naked, plaiting vines and with twigs in his hand."[15] Thoreau's rebellion seemed to Emerson too much a matter of denials. So it was, for the naturalist was not given time to work his way through to the affirmations concerning the conduct of life which he wished one day to make, and which he hoped to find in a study of nature. Fate overruled him. One day in the spring of the year 1862, when McClellan in Virginia was preparing his assault upon Richmond, Emerson wrote sadly in his *Journal*: "Sam Staples yes-

terday had been to see Henry Thoreau. 'Never spent an hour with more satisfaction. Never saw a man dying with so much pleasure and peace.'" On May 6 Thoreau passed, content with his denials and to leave the affirmations to other men.

Emerson and Thoreau lived in that epoch in which the American frontier was sweeping westward to the Pacific. On the edge of the wilderness, individualism was the normal and inevitable way of life. Here men, like Bill Williams, were free. Out of the frontier came American insistence upon personal liberty. But the freedom of Williams was that of escape. He abandoned a society whose growing complexity increased the problem of living. In the older communities, increase in numbers multiplied the restraints upon the individual man. The institutions which men established put them in shackles. The strong preyed upon the weak. For such problems the frontier, save only as it kept alive the ideal of the free individual, had no solution. It was a transient moment. And when it passed, the tasks of the East would become those of the West.

Emerson and Thoreau remained in New England in an environment in which, already, wealth was passing into the hands of the few. The rough equalitarianism of the frontier had long since disappeared. These two friends faced the issues of their day in the region where solutions were hardest to find. Both were dissenters. Their significance lay in the fact that they served as spokesmen for an emerging democratic faith and, in so doing, gave comfort to men groping for enlightenment in an era in which society was closing in upon the individual. Emerson taught the individual the nobility of himself, the divinity of the average

15 Perry, 238.

human. Thoreau insisted that the individual was right in his dissatisfaction with organized society, whether it was the college, the bank, the railroad, the Church, or the State. For both men the central problem was one of ethics, and the task of the moment was to make moral energy effective upon the earth. Both began with the doctrine of the fundamental law and interpreted it in ethical terms. Each insisted that human freedom is only achieved when men express, in their lives, that moral sentiment which permeates nature from the center of the cosmos to its circumference. Both were hopeful that the ideals of the democratic faith could be made to triumph over the materialism of American business and politics. Emerson expressed the mood of these two Concord rebels, who were carrying on the fight which had been started by the farmers at the bridge. "We are not minors and invalids," said the poet speaking for all Americans who venerated the idealism of democracy, "not cowards fleeing before a revolution, but guides, redeemers, benefactors, obeying the Almighty effort and advancing on Chaos and the Dark."[16]

16 R. W. Emerson, "Self-Reliance," *Complete Works*, II, 47.

Ralph Waldo Emerson:

THE TRANSCENDENTALIST

This essay of Emerson's is the best statement of what he meant by "transcendentalism." For him it is a generalized attitude taken by an individual toward nature and toward society. "I am," he said, "in all my theories, ethics and politics a poet." The poet's gift is his power of intuition, to perceive the ideal within the real. But this very "double consciousness," as Emerson called it, makes the more difficult for him any effort to cope with the exigencies and compromises of the workaday world: "It is simpler to be self-dependent." This is, then, for Emerson the transcendentalist's problem: What duty have these lonely ones to society and what are the duties of society in reference to them? It is the tormenting question he tries to answer in this essay — and that also inspired the Ode Inscribed to W. H. Channing.

THE first thing we have to say respecting what are called *new views* here in New England, at the present time, is, that they are not new, but the very oldest of thoughts cast into the mould of these new times. The light is always identical in its composition, but it falls on a great variety of objects, and by so falling is first revealed to us, not in its own form, for it is formless, but in theirs; in like manner, thought only appears in the objects it classifies. What is popularly called Transcendentalism among us, is Idealism; Idealism as it appears in 1842. As thinkers, mankind have ever divided into two sects, Materialists and Idealists; the first class founding on experience, the second on consciousness; the first class beginning to think from the data of the senses, the second class perceive that the senses are not final, and say, The senses give us representations of things, but what are the things themselves, they cannot tell. The materialist insists on facts, on history, on the force of circumstances and the animal wants of man; the idealist on the power of Thought and of Will, on inspiration, on miracle, on individual culture. These two modes of thinking are both natural, but the idealist contends that his way of thinking is in higher nature. He concedes all that the other affirms, admits the impressions of sense, admits their coherency, their use and beauty, and then asks the materialist for his grounds of assurance that things are as his senses represent them. But I, he says, affirm facts not affected by the illusions of sense, facts which are of the same nature as the faculty which reports them, and not liable to doubt; facts which in their first appearance to us assume a native superiority to material facts, regarding these into a language by which the first are to be spoken; facts which it only needs a retirement from the senses to discern. Every materialist will be an idealist; but an idealist can never go backward to be a materialist.

The idealist, in speaking of events, sees them as spirits. He does not deny the sensuous fact: by no means; but he will not see that alone. He does not deny the presence of this table, this chair, and the walls of this room, but he looks at these things as the reverse side of the tapestry, as the *other end,* each being a sequel or completion of a spiritual fact which nearly concerns him. This manner of looking at things transfers every object in nature from an independent and anoma-lous position without there, into the consciousness. Even the materialist Condillac, perhaps the most logical expounder of materialism, was constrained to say, "Though we should soar into the heavens, though we should sink into the abyss, we never go out of ourselves; it is always our own thought that we perceive." What more could an idealist say?

The materialist, secure in the certainty of sensation, mocks at fine-spun theories, at star-gazers and dreamers, and believes that his life is solid, that he at least takes nothing for granted, but knows where he stands, and what he does. Yet how easy it is to show him that he also is a phantom walking and working amid phantoms, and that he need only ask a question or two beyond his daily questions to find his solid universe growing dim and impalpable before his sense. The sturdy capitalist, no matter how deep and square on blocks of Quincy granite he lays the foundations of his banking-house or Exchange, must set it, at last, not on a cube corresponding to the angles of his structure, but on a mass of unknown materials and solidity, red-hot or white-hot perhaps at the core, which rounds off to an almost perfect sphericity, and lies floating in soft air, and goes spinning away, dragging bank and banker with it at a rate of thousands of miles the hour, he knows not whither, — a bit of bullet, now glimmering, now darkling through a small cubic space on the edge of an unimaginable pit of emptiness. And this wild balloon, in which his whole venture is embarked, is a just symbol of his whole state and faculty. One thing at least, he says, is certain, and does not give me the headache, that figures do not lie; the multiplication table has been hitherto found unimpeachable truth; and, moreover, if I put a gold eagle in my safe, I find it again to-morrow; — but for these thoughts, I know not whence they are. They change and pass away. But ask him why he believes that an uniform experience will continue uniform or on what grounds he founds his faith in his figures, and he will perceive that his mental fabric is built up on just as strange and quaking foundations as his proud edifice of stone.

In the order of thought, the materialist takes his departure from the external world, and esteems a man as one product of that. The idealist takes his departure from his consciousness, and reckons the world an appearance. The materialist respects sensible masses, Society, Government, social art and luxury, every establishment, every mass, whether majority of numbers, or extent of space, or amount of objects, every social action. The idealist has another measure, which is metaphysical, namely the *rank* which things themselves take in his consciousness; not at all the size or appearance. Mind is the only reality, of which men and all other natures are better or worse reflectors. Nature, literature, history, are only subjective phenomena. Although in his action overpowered by the laws of action, and so, warmly cooperating with men, even preferring them to himself, yet when he speaks scientifically, or after the order of thought, he is constrained to degrade persons into representatives of truths. He does not respect labor, or the products of labor, namely property, otherwise than as a manifold symbol, illustrating with wonderful fidelity of details the laws of being; he does not respect government, except as far as it reiterates the law of his mind; nor the church, nor charities, nor arts, for themselves; but hears, as at a vast distance, what they say, as if his consciousness would speak to him through a panto-mimic scene. His thought, — that is the Universe. His experience inclines him to behold the procession of facts you call the world, as flowing perpetually outward from an invisible, unsounded centre in himself, centre alike of him and of them, and necessitating him to regard all things as having a subjective or relative existence, relative to that aforesaid Unknown Centre of him.

From this transfer of the world into the consciousness, this beholding of all things in the mind, follow easily his whole ethics. It is simpler to be self-dependent. The height, the deity of man is to be self-sustained, to need no gift, no foreign force. Society is good when it does not violate me, but best when it is likest to solitude. Everything real is self-existent. Everything divine shares the self-existence of Deity. All that you call the world is the shadow of that substance which you are, the perpetual creation of the powers of thought, of those that are dependent and of those that are independent of your will. Do not cumber yourself with fruitless pains to mend and remedy remote effects; let the soul be erect, and all things will go well. You think me the child of my circumstances: I make my circumstance. Let any thought or motive of mine be different from that they are, the difference will transform my condition and economy. I — this thought which is called I — is the mould into which the world is poured like melted wax. The mould is invisible, but the world betrays the shape of the mould. You call it the power of circumstance, but it is the power of me. Am I in harmony with myself? my position will seem to you just and commanding. Am I vicious and insane? my fortunes will seem to you obscure and descending. As I am, so shall I associate, and so shall I act; Caesar's history will paint out Caesar. Jesus acted so, because he thought so. I do not wish to overlook or to gainsay any reality; I say I make my circumstance; but if you ask me, Whence am I? I feel like other men my relation to that Fact which cannot be spoken, or defined, nor even thought, but which exists, and will exist.

The Transcendentalist adopts the whole connection of spiritual doctrine. He believes in miracle, in the perpetual openness of the human mind to new influx of light and power; he believes in inspiration, and in ecstasy. He wishes that the spiritual principle should be suffered to demonstrate itself to the end, in all possible applications to the state of man, without the admission of anything unspiritual; that is, anything positive, dogmatic, personal. Thus the spiritual measure of inspiration is the depth of the thought, and never, who said it? And so he resists all attempts to palm other rules and measures on the spirit than its own.

In action he easily incurs the charge of antinomianism by his avowal that he, who has the Lawgiver, may with safety not only neglect, but even contravene every written commandment. In the play of Othello, the expiring Desdemona absolves her husband of the murder, to her attendant Emilia. Afterwards, when Emilia charges him with the crime, Othello exclaims, "You heard her say herself it was not I." Emilia replies, "The more angel she, and thou the blacker devil."

Of this fine incident, Jacobi, the Transcendental moralist, makes use, with other parallel instances, in his reply to Fichte. Jacobi, refusing all measure of right and wrong except the determinations of the private spirit, remarks that there is no crime but has sometimes been a virtue. "I," he says, "am that atheist, that godless person who, in opposition to an imaginary doctrine of calculation, would lie as the dying Desdemona lied; would lie and deceive, as Pylades when he personated Orestes; would assassinate like Timoleon; would perjure myself like Epaminondas and John de Witt; I would resolve on suicide like Cato; I would commit sacrilege with David; yea, and pluck ears of corn on the Sabbath, for no other reason than that I was fainting for lack of food. For I have assurance in myself that in pardoning these faults according to the letter, man exerts the sovereign right which the majesty of his being confers on him; he sets the seal of his divine nature to the grace he accords."

In like manner, if there is anything grand and daring in human thought or virtue, any reliance on the vast, the unknown; any presentiment, any extravagance of faith, the spiritualist adopts it as most in nature. The oriental mind has always tended to this largeness. Buddhism is an expression of it. The Buddhist, who thanks no man, who says "Do not flatter your benefactors," but who, in his conviction that every good deed can by no possibility escape its reward, will not deceive the benefactor by pretending that he has done more than he should, is a Transcendentalist.

You will see by this sketch that there is no such thing as a Transcendental *party*; that there is no pure Transcendentalist; that we know of none but prophets and heralds of such a philosophy; that all who by strong bias of nature have leaned to the spiritual side in doctrine, have stopped short of their goal. We have had many harbingers and forerunners; but of a purely spiritual life, history has afforded no example. I mean we have yet no man who has leaned entirely on his character, and eaten angels' food; who, trusting to his sentiments, found life made of miracles; who, working for universal aims, found himself fed, he knew not how; clothed, sheltered, and weaponed, he knew not how, and yet it was done by his own hands. Only in the instinct of the lower animals we find the suggestion of the methods of it, and something higher than our understanding. The squirrel hoards nuts and the bee gathers honey, without knowing what they do, and they are thus provided for without selfishness or disgrace.

Shall we say then that Transcendentalism is the Saturnalia or excess of Faith; the presentiment of a faith proper to man in his integrity, excessive only when his imperfect obedience hinders the satisfaction of his wish? Nature is transcendental, exists primarily, necessarily, ever works and advances, yet takes no thought for the morrow. Man owns the dignity of the life which throbs around him, in chemistry, and tree, and animal, and in the involuntary functions of his own body; yet he is balked when he tries to fling himself into this enchanted circle, where all is done without degradation. Yet genius and virtue predict in man the same absence of private ends and of condescension to circumstances, united with every trait and talent of beauty and power.

This way of thinking, falling on Roman times, made Stoic philosophers; falling on despotic times, made patriot Catos and Brutuses; falling on superstitious times, made prophets and apostles; on popish times, made protestants and ascetic monks, preachers of Faith against the preachers of Works; on prelatical times, made Puritans and Quakers; and falling on Unitarian and commercial times, makes the peculiar shades of Idealism which we know.

It is well known to most of my audience that the Idealism of the present day acquired the name of Transcendental from the use of that term by Immanuel Kant, of Königsberg, who replied to the skeptical philosophy of Locke, which insisted that there was nothing in the intellect which was not previously in the experience of the senses, by showing that there was a very important class of ideas or imperative forms, which did not come by experience, but through which experience was acquired; that these were intuitions of the mind itself; and he denominated them *Transcendental* forms. The extraordinary profoundness and precision of that man's thinking have given vogue to his nomenclature, in Europe and America, to that extent that whatever belongs to the class of intuitive thought is popularly called at the present day *Transcendental*.

Although, as we have said, there is no pure Transcendentalist, yet the tendency to respect the intuitions and to give them, at least in our creed, all authority over our experience, has deeply colored the conversation and poetry of the present day; and the history of genius and of religion in these times, though impure, and as yet not incarnated in any powerful individual, will be the history of this tendency.

It is a sign of our times, conspicuous to the coarsest observer, that many intelligent and religious persons withdraw themselves from the common labors and competitions of the market and the caucus, and betake themselves to a certain solitary and critical way of living, from which no solid fruit has yet appeared to justify their separation. They hold themselves aloof: they feel the disproportion between their faculties and the work offered them, and they prefer to ramble in the country and perish of ennui, to the degradation of such charities and such ambitions as the city can propose to them. They are striking work, and crying out for somewhat worthy to do! What they do is done only because they are overpowered by the humanities that speak on all sides; and they consent to such labor as is open to them, though to their lofty dream the writing of Iliads or Hamlets, or the building of cities or empires seems drudgery.

Now every one must do after his kind, be he asp or angel, and these must. The question which a wise man and a student of modern history will ask, is, what that kind is? And truly, as in ecclesiastical history we take so much pains to know what the Gnostics, what the Essenes, what the Manichees, and what the Reformers believed, it would not misbecome us to inquire nearer home, what these companions and contemporaries of ours think and do, at least so far as these thoughts and actions appear to be not accidental and personal, but common to many, and the inevitable flower of the Tree of Time. Our American literature and spiritual history are, we confess, in the optative mood; but whoso knows these seething brains, these admirable radicals, these unsocial worshippers, these talkers who talk the sun and moon away, will believe that this heresy cannot pass away without leaving its mark.

They are lonely; the spirit of their writing and conversation is lonely; they repel influences; they shun general society; they incline to shut themselves in their chamber in the house, to live in the country rather than in the town, and to find their tasks and amusements in solitude. Society, to be sure, does not like this very well; it saith, Whoso goes to walk alone, accuses the whole world; he declares all to be unfit to be his companions; it is very uncivil, nay, insulting; Society will retaliate. Meantime, this retirement does not proceed from any whim on the part of these separators; but if any one will take pains to talk with them, he will find that this part is chosen both from temperament and from principle; with some unwillingness too, and as a choice of the less of two evils; for these persons are not by nature melancholy, sour, and unsocial, — they are not stockish or brute, — but joyous, susceptible, affectionate; they have even more than others a great wish to be loved. Like the young Mozart, they are rather ready to cry ten times a day, "But are you sure you love me?" Nay, if they tell you their whole thought, they will own that love seems to them the last and highest gift of nature; that there are persons whom in their hearts they daily thank for existing, — persons whose faces are perhaps unknown to them, but whose fame and spirit have penetrated their solitude, — and for whose sake they wish to exist. To behold the beauty of another character, which inspires a new interest in our own; to behold the beauty lodged in a human being, with such vivacity of apprehension that I am instantly forced home to inquire if I am not deformity itself; to behold in another the expression of a love so high that it assures itself, — assures itself also to me against every possible casualty except my unworthiness; — these are degrees on the scale of human happiness to which they have ascended; and it is a fidelity to this sentiment which has made common association distasteful to them. They wish a just and even fellowship, or none. They cannot gossip with you, and they do not wish, as they are sincere and religious, to gratify any mere curiosity which you may entertain. Like fairies, they do not wish to be spoken of. Love me, they say, but do not ask who is my cousin and my uncle. If you do not need to hear my thought, because you can read it in my face and behavior, then I will tell it you from sunrise to sunset. If you cannot divine it, you would not understand what I say. I will not molest myself for you. I do not wish to be profaned.

And yet, it seems as if this loneliness, and not this love, would prevail in their circumstances, because of the extravagant demand they make on human nature. That, indeed, constitutes a new feature in their portrait, that they are the most exacting and extortionate critics. Their quarrel with every man they meet is not with his kind, but with his degree. There is not enough of him, — that is the only fault. They prolong their privilege of childhood in this wise; of doing nothing, but making immense demands on all the gladiators in the lists of action and fame. They make us feel the strange disappointment which overcasts every human youth. So many promising youths, and never a finished man! The profound nature will have a savage rudeness; the delicate one will be shallow, or the victim of sensibility; the richly accomplished will have some capital absurdity; and so every piece has a crack. 'Tis strange, but this masterpiece is the result of such an extreme delicacy that the most unobserved flaw in the boy will neutralize the most aspiring genius, and spoil the work. Talk with a seaman of the hazards to life in his profession and he will ask you. "Where are the old sailors? Do you not see that all are young men?" And we, on this sea of human thought, in like manner inquire, Where are the old idealists? where are they who represented to the last generation that extravagant hope which a few happy aspirants suggest to ours? In looking at the class of counsel, and power, and wealth, and at the matronage of the land, amidst all the prudence and all the triviality, one asks, Where are they who represented genius, virtue, the invisible and heavenly world, to these? Are they dead, — taken in early ripeness to the gods, — as ancient wisdom foretold their fate? Or did the high idea die out of them, and leave their unperfumed body as its tomb and tablet, announcing to all that the celestial inhabitant, who once gave them beauty, had departed? Will it be better with the new generation? We easily predict a fair future to each new candidate who enters the lists, but we are frivolous and volatile, and by low aims and ill example do what we can to defeat this hope. Then these youths bring us a rough but effectual aid. By their unconcealed dissatisfaction they expose our poverty and the insignificance of man to man. A man is a poor limitary benefactor. He ought to be a shower of benefits — a great influence, which should never let his brother go, but should refresh old merits continually with new ones; so that though absent he should never be out of my mind, his name never far from my lips; but if the earth should open at my side, or my last hour were come, his name should be the prayer I should utter to the Universe. But in our experience, man is cheap and friendship wants its deep sense. We affect to dwell with our friends in their absence, but we do not; when deed, word, or letter comes not, they let us go. These exacting children advertise us of our wants. There is no compliment, no smooth speech with them; they pay you only this one compliment, of insatiable expectation; they aspire, they severely exact, and if they only stand fast in this watch-tower, and persist in demanding unto the end, and without end, then are they terrible friends, whereof poet and priest cannot choose but stand in awe; and what if

they eat clouds, and drink wind, they
have not been without service to the
race of man.

With this passion for what is great and
extraordinary, it cannot be wondered at
that they are repelled by vulgarity and
frivolity in people. They say to themselves, It is better to be alone than in
bad company. And it is really a wish to
be met, — the wish to find society for
their hope and religion, — which prompts
them to shun what is called society. They
feel that they are never so fit for friendship as when they have quitted mankind
and taken themselves to friend. A picture, a book, a favorite spot in the hills
or the woods which they can people with
the fair and worthy creation of the fancy,
can give them often forms so vivid that
these for the time shall seem real, and
society the illusion.

But their solitary and fastidious manners not only withdraw them from the
conversation, but from the labors of the
world; they are not good citizens, not
good members of society; unwillingly
they bear their part of the public and
private burdens; they do not willingly
share in the public charities, in the public religious rites, in the enterprises of
education, of missions foreign and do-
mestic, in the abolition of the slave-trade,
or in the temperance society. They do
not even like to vote. The philanthropists
inquire whether Transcendentalism does
not mean sloth: they had as lief hear
that their friend is dead, as that he is a
Transcendentalist; for then is he para-
lyzed, and can never do anything for
humanity. What right, cries the good
world, has the man of genius to retreat
from work, and indulge himself? The
popular literary creed seems to be, "'I am
a sublime genius; I ought not therefore
to labor." But genius is the power to
labor better and more availably. Deserve

thy genius: exalt it. The good, the illu-
minated, sit apart from the rest, censuring
their dulness and vices, as if they thought
that by sitting very grand in their chairs,
the very brokers, attorneys, and congress-
men would see the error of their ways,
and flock to them. But the good and wise
must learn to act, and carry salvation to
the combatants and demagogues in the
dusty arena below.

On the part of these children it is replied that life and their faculty seem to
them gifts too rich to be squandered on
such trifles as you propose to them. What
you call your fundamental institutions,
your great and holy causes, seem to them
great abuses, and, when nearly seen,
paltry matters. Each "cause" as it is
called, — say Abolition, Temperance, say
Calvinism, or Unitarianism, — becomes
speedily a little shop, where the article,
let it have been at first never so subtle
and ethereal, is now made up into portable and convenient cakes, and retailed
in small quantities to suit purchasers.
You make very free use of these words
"great" and "holy," but few things appear to them such. Few persons have
any magnificence of nature to inspire
enthusiasm, and the philanthropies and
charities have a certain air of quackery.
As to the general course of living, and
the daily employments of men, they cannot see much virtue in these, since they
are parts of this vicious circle; and as no
great ends are answered by the men,
there is nothing noble in the arts by
which they are maintained. Nay, they
have made the experiment and found that
from the liberal professions to the coarsest manual labor, and from the cour-
tesies of the academy and the college
to the conventions of the cotillon-room
and the morning call, there is a spirit
of cowardly compromise and seeming
which intimates a frightful skepticism, a

life without love, and an activity without an aim.

Unless the action is necessary, unless it is adequate, I do not wish to perform it. I do not wish to do one thing but once. I do not love routine. Once possessed of the principle, it is equally easy to make four or forty thousand applications of it. A great man will be content to have indicated in any the slightest manner his perception of the reigning Idea of his time, and will leave to those who like it the multiplication of examples. When he has hit the white, the rest may shatter the target. Every thing admonishes us how needlessly long life is. Every moment of a hero so raises and cheers us that a twelve-month is an age. All that the brave Xanthus brings home from his wars is the recollection that at the storming of Samos, "in the heat of the battle, Pericles smiled on me, and passed on to another detachment." It is the quality of the moment, not the number of days, of events, or of actors, that imoprts.

New, we confess, and by no means happy, is our condition: if you want the aid of our labor, we ourselves stand in greater want of the labor. We are miserable with inaction. We perish of rest and rust: but we do not like your work.

"Then," says the world, "show me your own."

"We have none."

"What will you do, then?" cries the world.

"We will wait."

"How long?"

"Until the Universe beckons and calls us to work."

"But whilst you wait, you grow old and useless."

"Be it so: I can sit in a corner and *perish* (as you call it), but I will not move until I have the highest command. If no call should come for years, for centuries, then I know that the want of the Universe is the attestation of faith by my abstinence. Your virtuous projects, so called, do not cheer me. I know that which shall come will cheer me. If I cannot work at least I need not lie. All that is clearly due to-day is not to lie. In other places other men have encountered sharp trials, and have behaved themselves well. The martyrs were sawn asunder, or hung alive on meathooks. Cannot we screw our courage to patience and truth, and without complaints, or even with good-humor, await our turn of action in the Infinite Counsels?"

But to come a little closer to the secret of these persons, we must say that to them it seems a very easy matter to answer the objections of the man of the world, but not so easy to dispose of the doubts and objections that occur to themselves. They are exercised in their own spirit with queries which acquaint them with all adversity, and with the trials of the bravest heroes. When I asked them concerning their private experience, they answered somewhat in this wise: It is not to be denied that there must be some wide difference between my faith and other faith; and mine is a certain brief experience, which surprised me in the highway or in the market, in some place, at some time, — whether in the body or out of the body, God knoweth, — and made me aware that I had played the fool with fools all this time, but that law existed for me and for all; that to me belonged trust, a child's trust and obedience, and the worship of ideas, and I should never be fool more. Well, in the space of an hour probably, I was let down from this height; I was at my old tricks, the selfish member of a selfish society. My life is superficial, takes no root in the deep world; I ask, When shall

I die and be relieved of the responsibility of seeing an Universe which I do not use? I wish to exchange this flash-of-lightning faith for continuous daylight, this fever-glow for a benign climate.

These two states of thought diverge every moment, and stand in wild contrast. To him who looks at his life from these moments of illumination, it will seem that he skulks and plays a mean, shiftless and subaltern part in the world. That is to be done which he has not skill to do, or to be said which others can say better, and he lies by, or occupies his hands with some plaything, until his hour comes again. Much of our reading, much of our labor, seems mere waiting: it was not that we were born for. Any other could do it as well or better. So little skill enters into these works, so little do they mix with the divine life, that it really signifies little what we do, whether we turn a grindstone, or ride, or run, or make fortunes, or govern the state. The worst feature of this double consciousness is, that the two lives, of the understanding and of the soul, which we lead, really show very little relation to each other; never meet and measure each other: one prevails now, all buzz and din; and the other prevails then, all infinitude and paradise; and, with the progress of life, the two discover no greater disposition to reconcile themselves. Yet, what is my faith? What am I? What but a thought of serenity and independence, an abode in the deep blue sky? Presently the clouds shut down again; yet we retain the belief that this petty web we weave will at last be overshot and reticulated with veins of the blue, and that the moments will characterize the days. Patience, then, is for us, is it not? Patience, and still patience. When we pass, as presently we shall, into some new infinitude, out of this Iceland of negations, it will please us to reflect that though we had few virtues or consolations, we bore with our indigence, nor once strove to repair it with hypocrisy or false heat of any kind.

But this class are not sufficiently characterized if we omit to add that they are lovers and worshippers of Beauty. In the eternal trinity of Truth, Goodness, and Beauty, each in its perfection including the three, they prefer to make Beauty the sign and head. Something of the same taste is observable in all the moral movements of the time, in the religious and benevolent enterprises. They have a liberal, even an aesthetic spirit. A reference to Beauty in action sounds to be sure a little hollow and ridiculous in the ears of the old church. In politics, it has often sufficed, when they treated of justice, if they kept the bounds of selfish calculation. If they granted restitution, it was prudence which granted it. But the justice which is now claimed for the black, and the pauper, and the drunkard, is for Beauty, — is for a necessity to the soul of the agent, not of the beneficiary. I say this is the tendency, not yet the realization. Our virtue totters and trips, does not yet walk firmly. Its representatives are austere; they preach and denounce; their rectitude is not yet a grace. They are still liable to that slight taint of burlesque which in our strange world attaches to the zealot. A saint should be as dear as the apple of the eye. Yet we are tempted to smile, and we flee from the working to the speculative reformer, to escape that same slight ridicule. Alas for these days of derision and criticism! We call the Beautiful the highest, because it appears to us the golden mean, escaping the dowdiness of the good and the heartlessness of the true. They are lovers of nature also, and find an indemnity in the inviolable order of the world for the violated order and grace of man.

There is, no doubt, a great deal of well-founded objection to be spoken or felt against the sayings and doings of this class, some of whose traits we have selected; no doubt they will lay themselves open to criticism and to lampoons, and as ridiculous stories will be to be told of them as of any. There will be cant and pretension; there will be subtilty and moonshine. These persons are of unequal strength, and do not all prosper. They complain that everything around them must be denied; and if feeble, it takes all their strength to deny, before they can begin to lead their own life. Grave seniors insist on their respect to this institution and that usage; to an obsolete history; to some vocation, or college, or etiquette, or beneficiary, or charity, or morning or evening call, which they resist as what does not concern them. But it costs such sleepless nights, alienations and misgivings, — they have so many moods about it; these old guardians never change *their* minds; they have but one mood on the subject, namely, that Antony is very perverse, — that it is quite as much as Antony can do to assert his rights, abstain from what he thinks foolish, and keep his temper. He cannot help the reaction of this injustice in his own mind. He is braced-up and stilted; all freedom and flowing genius, all sallies of wit and frolic nature are quite out of the question; it is well if he can keep from lying, injustice, and suicide. This is no time for gaiety and grace. His strength and spirits are wasted in rejection. But the strong spirits overpower those around them without effort. Their thought and emotion comes in like a flood, quite withdraws them from all notice of these carping critics; they surrender themselves with glad heart to the heavenly guide,

and only by implication reject the clamorous nonsense of the hour. Grave seniors talk to the deaf, — church and old book mumble and ritualize to an unheeding, preoccupied and advancing mind, and thus they by happiness of greater momentum lose no time, but take the right road at first.

But all these of whom I speak are not proficients; they are novices; they only show the road in which man should travel, when the soul has greater health and prowess. Yet let them feel the dignity of their charge, and deserve a larger power. Their heart is the ark in which the fire is concealed which shall burn in a broader and universal flame. Let them obey the Genius then most when his impulse is wildest; then most when he seems to lead to uninhabitable deserts of thought and life; for the path which the hero travels alone is the highway of health and benefit to mankind. What is the privilege and nobility of our nature but its persistency, through its power to attach itself to what is permanent?

Society also has its duties in reference to this class, and must behold them with what charity it can. Possibly some benefit may yet accrue from them to the state. In our Mechanics' Fair, there must be not only bridges, ploughs, carpenters' planes, and baking troughs, but also some few finer instruments, — rain gauges, thermometers, and telescopes; and in society, besides farmers, sailors, and weavers, there must be a few persons of purer fire kept specially as gauges and meters of character; persons of a fine, detecting instinct, who note the smallest accumulations of wit and feeling in the bystander. Perhaps too there might be room for the exciters and monitors; collectors of the heavenly spark, with power to convey the electricity to others. Or, as the storm-tossed vessel at sea speaks the

frigate or "line packet" to learn its longi-
tude, so it may not be without its advantage that we should now and then en-
counter rare and gifted men, to compare
the points of our spiritual compass, and
verify our bearings from superior
chronometers.

Amidst the downward tendency and
proneness of things, when every voice is
raised for a new road or another statute
or a subscription of stock; for an improvement in dress, or in dentistry; for
a new house or a larger business; for a
political party, or the division of an
estate; — will you not tolerate one or two
solitary voices in the land, speaking for
thoughts and principles not marketable
or perishable? Soon these improvements
and mechanical inventions will be super-
seded; these modes of living lost out of
memory; these cities rotted, ruined by
war, by new inventions, by new seats of
trade, or the geologic changes: — all
gone, like the shells which sprinkle the
sea-beach with a white colony to-day,
forever renewed to be forever destroyed.
But the thoughts which these few her-
mits strove to proclaim by silence as well
as by speech, not only by what they did,
but by what they forebore to do, shall
abide in beauty and strength, to reorgan-
ize themselves in nature, to invest themselves anew in other, perhaps higher
endowed and happier mixed clay than
ours, in fuller union with the surrounding
system.

Ralph Waldo Emerson: ODE INSCRIBED TO
W. H. CHANNING

Though loath to grieve
The evil time's sole patriot,
I cannot leave
My honied thought
For the priest's cant,
Or statesman's rant.

If I refuse
My study for their politique,
Which at the best is trick,
The angry Muse
Puts confusion in my brain.

But who is he that prates
Of the culture of mankind,
Of better arts and life?
Go, blindworm, go
Behold the famous States
Harrying Mexico
With rifle and with knife!

Or who, with accent bolder,
Dare praise the freedom-loving mountaineer?
I found by thee, O rushing Contoocook!
And in thy valleys, Agiochook!
The jackals of the Negro-holder.

The God who made New Hampshire
Taunted the lofty land
With little men; —
Small bat and wren

House in the oak: —
If earth-fire cleave
The unheaved land, and bury the folk,
The southern crocodile would grieve.
Virtue palters; Right is hence;
Freedom praised, but hid;
Funeral eloquence
Rattles the coffin-lid.

What boots thy zeal,
O glowing friend,
That would indignant rend
The northland from the south?
Wherefore? to what good end?
Boston Bay and Bunker Hill
Would serve things still; —
Things are of the snake.

The horseman serves the horse,
The neatherd serves the neat,
The merchant serves the purse,
The eater serves his meat;
'T is the day of the chattel,
Web to weave, and corn to grind;
Things are in the saddle,
And ride mankind.

There are two laws discrete,
Not reconciled, —
Law for man, and law for thing;
The last builds town and fleet,
But it runs wild,
And doth the man unking.

'T is fit the forest fall
The steep be graded,
The mountain tunnelled,
The sand shaded,
The orchard planted,
The glebe tilled,
The prairie granted,
The steamer built.

Let man serve law for man:
Live for friendship, live for love,
For truth's and harmony's behoof;
The state may follow how it can,
As Olympus follows Jove.

Yet do not I implore
The wrinkled shopman to my sounding
          woods,
Nor bid the unwilling senator
Ask votes of thrushes in the solitudes.
Every one to his chosen work; —
Foolish hands may mix and mar;
Wise and sure the issues are.
Round they roll till dark is light,
Sex to sex, and even to odd; —
The over-god
Who Marries Right to Might,
Who peoples, unpeoples, —
He who exterminates
Races by stronger races,
Black by white faces, —
Knows to bring honey
Out of the lion;
Grafts gentlest scion
On pirate and Turk.

The Cossack eats Poland,
Like stolen fruit;
Her last noble is ruined,
Her last poet mute:
Straight, into double band
The victors divide;
Half for freedom strike and stand; —
The astonished Muse finds thousands at her
          side.

Nathaniel Hawthorne: BROOK FARM

The 1840's were a decade of intense social ferment during which a great number of utopian communities both secular and religious were established. The transcendentalists in their various ways responded to the mood of the time. Emerson wrote to Carlyle: "We are all a little wild here with numberless projects of social reform. Not a reading man but has a draft of a new community in his pocket. . . George Ripley is talking up a colony of agriculturists and scholars with whom he threatens to take the field and the book." Brook Farm, founded under Ripley's leadership in 1841, was like nearly all the others an attempt to solve the problem of relating manual work to culture. Bronson Alcott's abortive little community, Fruitlands, and Thoreau's "experiment of living" at Walden were similarly motivated. Emerson, for whom at "the name of a society all my repulsions play, all my quills rise and sharpen," remained the benevolently neutral observer.

Hawthorne, far more detached and skeptical than Emerson, was no transcendentalist. He joined Brook Farm for a practical reason. His work as a measurer at the Boston customhouse was wearisome and prevented him from achieving what he wanted to do as a writer. Nor was he as yet in a financial position to marry Sophia Peabody. Brook Farm seemed the way to satisfy both needs. These amusingly ironic comments on what he later described as "certainly the most romantic episode of my own life" record his disillusionment.

Brook Farm, Oak Hill, April 13th, 1841. — . . . I have not yet taken my first lesson in agriculture, except that I went to see our cows foddered, yesterday afternoon. We have eight of our own; and the number is now increased by a transcendental heifer belonging to Miss Margaret Fuller. She is very fractious, I believe, and apt to kick over the milk-pail. . . . I intend to convert myself into a milkmaid this evening, but I pray Heaven that Mr. Ripley may be moved to assign me the kindliest cow in the herd, otherwise I shall perform my duty with fear and trembling.

I like my brethren in affliction very well; and, could you see us sitting round our table at meal-times, before the great kitchen fire, you would call it a cheerful sight. Mrs. B—— is a most comfortable woman to behold. She looks as if her ample person were stuffed full of tenderness, — indeed, as if she were all one great, kind heart.

April 14th, 10 A. M. — . . . I did not milk the cows last night, because Mr. Ripley was afraid to trust them to my hands, or me to their horns, I know not which. But this morning I have done wonders. Before breakfast, I went out to the barn and began to chop hay for the cattle, and with such "righteous vehemence," as Mr. Ripley says, did I labor, that in the space of ten minutes I broke the machine. Then I brought wood and replenished the fires; and finally went down to breakfast, and ate up a huge

From *The American Notebooks* (Houghton Mifflin and Co., Cambridge, Mass., 1896), pp. 227–238.

mound of buckwheat cakes. After breakfast, Mr. Ripley put a four-pronged instrument into my hands, which he gave
me to understand was called a pitchfork;
and he and Mr. Farley being armed with
similar weapons, we all three commenced
a gallant attack upon a heap of manure.
This office being concluded, and I having
purified myself, I sit down to finish this
letter. . . .

Miss Fuller's cow hooks the other cows,
and has made herself ruler of the herd,
and behaves in a very tyrannical manner. . . . I shall make an excellent husbandman, — I feel the original Adam re-
viving within me.

April 16th. — . . . I have milked a
cow! ! ! . . . The herd has rebelled against
the usurpation of Miss Fuller's heifer;
and, whenever they are turned out of the
barn, she is compelled to take refuge
under our protection. So much did she
impede my labors by keeping close to
me, that I found it necessary to give her
two or three gentle pats with a shovel;
but still she preferred to trust herself to
my tender mercies, rather than venture
among the horns of the herd. She is not
an amiable cow; but she has a very intelligent face, and seems to be of a re-
flective cast of character. I doubt not
that she will soon perceive the expediency of being on good terms with the
rest of the sisterhood.

I have not yet been twenty yards from
our house and barn; but I begin to perceive that this is a beautiful place. The
scenery is of a mild and placid character,
with nothing bold in its aspect; but I
think its beauties will grow upon us, and
make us love it the more, the longer we
live here. There is a brook, so near the
house that we shall be able to hear its
ripple in the summer evenings, . . . but,
for agricultural purposes, it has been

made to flow in a straight and rectangu-
lar fashion, which does it infinite damage
as a picturesque object. . . .

Mr. Ripley has bought four black pigs.

April 22d — . . . What an abominable
hand do I scribble! but I have been chop-
ping wood, and turning a grindstone all
the forenoon; and such occupations are
likely to disturb the equilibrium of the
muscles and sinews. It is an endless surprise to me how much work there is to
be done in the world; but, thank God,
I am able to do my share of it, — and
my ability increases daily. What a great,
broad-shouldered, elephantine personage
I shall become by and by!

May 4th. — . . . My cold no longer
troubles me, and all the morning I have
been at work under the clear, blue sky,
on a hill-side. Sometimes it almost
seemed as if I were at work in the sky
itself, though the material in which I
wrought was the ore from our gold-mine.
Nevertheless, there is nothing so un-
seemly and disagreeable in this sort of
toil as you could think. It defiles the
hands, indeed, but not the soul. This
gold ore is a pure and wholesome substance, else our mother Nature would not
devour it so readily, and derive so much
nourishment from it, and return such a
rich abundance of good grain and roots
in requital of it. . .

The farm is growing very beautiful
now, — not that we yet see anything of
the peas and potatoes which we have
planted; but the grass blushes green on
the slopes and hollows. I wrote that
word "blush" almost unconsciously; so we
will let it go as an inspired utterance. . . .

June 1st. — . . . I have been too busy
to write a long letter by this opportunity,
for I think this present life of mine gives

me an antipathy to pen and ink, even more than my Custom House experience did. . . . In the midst of toil, or after a hard day's work in the gold-mine, my soul obstinately refuses to be poured out on paper. That abominable gold-mine! Thank God, we anticipate getting rid of its treasures in the course of two or three days! Of all hateful places that is the worst, and I shall never comfort myself for having spent so many days of blessed sunshine there. It is my opinion that a man's soul may be buried and perish under a dung-heap, or in a furrow of the field, just as well as under a pile of money.

Mr. George Bradford will probably be here to-day, so that there will be no danger of my being under the necessity of laboring more than I like hereafter. Meantime my health is perfect, and my spirits buoyant, even in the gold-mine.

August 12th. — . . . I am very well, and not at all weary, for yesterday's rain gave us a holiday; and, moreover, the labors of the farm are not so pressing as they have been. And, joyful thought! in a little more than a fortnight I shall be free from my bondage, — . . . free to enjoy Nature, — free to think and feel! . . . Even my Custom House experience was not such a thraldom and weariness; my mind and heart were free. Oh, labor is the curse of the world, and nobody can meddle with it without becoming proportionably brutified! Is it a praiseworthy matter that I have spent five golden months in providing food for cows and horses? It is not so. . . .

Salem, September 3d. — . . . But really I should judge it to be twenty years since I left Brook Farm; and I take this to be one proof that my life there was an unnatural and unsuitable, and therefore an unreal, one. It already looks like a dream behind me. The real Me was never an associate of the community; there has been a spectral Appearance there, sounding the horn at daybreak, and milking the cows, and hoeing potatoes, and raking hay, toiling in the sun, and doing me the honor to assume my name. But this spectre was not myself. Nevertheless, it is somewhat remarkable that my hands have, during the past summer, grown very brown and rough, insomuch that many people persist in believing that I, after all, was the aforesaid spectral horn-sounder, cow-milker, potato-hoer, and hay-raker. But such people do not know a reality from a shadow. Enough of nonsense. I know not exactly how soon I shall return to the farm. Perhaps not sooner than a fortnight from to-morrow.

James Truslow Adams: EMERSON RE-READ

The late James Truslow Adams was one of the most prolific of American historians. He was editor-in-chief of the Dictionary of American History, *and author of an important series of volumes dealing with the history of New England.*

In this provocative article he develops the criticism made by Schlesinger of Emerson's attitude toward social and political affairs. Schlesinger accused Emerson of irresponsibility, asserting that he could "accept the status of citizenship . . . and dally with its obligations." Adams says that is so, and that it is so is due to the fact that his doctrine contains two great flaws: positively, he makes life too easy by his insistence on intuition and spontaneity; and negatively, his "shallow optimism" encourages us to behave with "the nonchalance of boys sure of a dinner." This sort of idealism, though it supports the generous illusions of youth, seems not just callow but dangerous to the soberly realistic and disillusioned man.

EXCEPT in tales of romance it is not given to us to be able to pass through postern doors or forest glades and find ourselves in lands of leisure where it is always afternoon. If one seeks the King of Elfland's Daughter it must be between the pages of a book. Nevertheless, one can change one's stage and ways of life and amplify one's days. Some months ago by a simple shift in space I so wrought a change in time that, for a while at least, I have been able without sense of haste or pressure to browse again among the books I read and marked as a boy, books which for more years than I like to count had stood untouched upon my shelves, open apparently to the reaching hand, but in reality, owing to lack of time, as remote as boyhood's days themselves.

A week ago, I picked up one of the oldest of these, oldest in possession, not in imprint — the *Essays* of Emerson. In an unformed hand there was the inscription on the flyleaf, "James Truslow Adams, 1896." I was then seventeen, and had evidently read him earlier, for at the beginning of a number of the essays, notably "Self-Reliance," are marked the dates of reading, "1895, '96, '96, '96." The volume, one of that excellent, well-printed series which in those halcyon days the National Book Company used to sell for fifty cents, is underlined and marked with marginal notes all through. The passages are not all those I should mark to-day, but at sixteen and seventeen it is clear I was reading Emerson with great enthusiasm, and again and again.

In the past few days I have gone through five volumes of his work and found the task no light one. What, I ask myself, is the trouble? It is obviously not that Emerson is not "modern," for the other evening I read aloud, to the mutual enjoyment of my wife and myself, the *Prometheus Chained* of Æschylus, which antedates Emerson by some twenty-five hundred years. I turn to Paul

Reprinted by permission from the *Atlantic Monthly*, 146 (October, 1930), 484–492.

More's *Shelburne Essays*, Volume XI, and read the statement that "it becomes more and more apparent that Emerson, judged by an international or even by a true national standard, is the outstanding figure of American letters."

I pause and ponder. "International," even "true national," standards are high. Whom have we? Lowell as a critic? One thinks of, say, Sainte-Beuve, and a shoulder shrug for Lowell. Lowell as poet, Whittier, Longfellow, Bryant? *Exeunt omnes*, except as second-rate by world standards. The troop of current novelists and poets are much the same here as in a half-dozen other countries. Hawthorne? A very distinctive, and yet a minor voice, in the international choir. Poe? Again a minor, and scarcely distinguishable as a "national." Whitman? One thinks of Whitman five hundred years hence in world terms, and shakes one's head. The choice is narrowing fast. Is Mr. More right? Yet the Emerson who evidently so stirred me at sixteen leaves me cold to-day at fifty. It is something to be looked into. I try, at fifty, to reappraise my Emerson. I take up the volumes again to see wherein the trouble lies.

First of all it occurs to me to test him by his own appraisals of others, and I turn to his volume on *Representative Men*. The list of names is itself of considerable significance — Plato, Swedenborg, Montaigne, Shakespeare, Napoleon, Goethe. Four of these are evidently so obvious as to tell us nothing of the mind choosing them. The case is a good deal like that of the Pulitzer Jury in biography, which is forbidden to award prizes for lives of Lincoln or Washington. The essential point is, what has Emerson to say of these men?

I confess that, when after these thirty years or more I turn from reading about Emerson to reading him himself, I am rather amazed by what seems to me the shallowness of these essays. In fact, I believe that even Mr. More considers the Plato a very unsatisfactory performance. Emerson babbles of "the Franklin-like wisdom" of Socrates, and, indeed, I think we could look for as sound an essay from an intelligent undergraduate. The Shakespeare is almost equally naïve and unsatisfying, and Emerson's final judgment is that the dramatist was merely a "master of the revels to mankind," the purveyor of "very superior pyrotechny this evening," and that the end of the record must be that with all his ability he "led an obscure and a profane life, using his genius for the public amusement." This essay throws much light on Emerson if little on Shakespeare. Nor does he show more real understanding of his other great men. He can say that Napoleon left no trace whatever on Europe, that "all passed away like the smoke of his artillery." Of Goethe's greatest poem, the *Faust*, Emerson notes mainly its "superior intelligence." One suspects that he chose these four names unconsciously because they were high in the world's record of the great, not because he understood the men or their work.

When he turns from these names, almost imposed upon him, to another of his independent choosing, it is illuminating that the one he dwells on with greatest admiration is Swedenborg. This fact is significant. For him, the Swedish mystic is "a colossal soul," the "last Father in the Church," "not likely to have a successor," compared with whom Plato is a "gownsman," whereas Lycurgus and Caesar would have to bow before the Swede. Emerson quotes from him as "golden sayings" such sentences as "in heaven the angels are advancing continually to the spring-time of their youth, so that the oldest angel appears the youngest," or "it is never permitted to any one in heaven, to stand behind another and look at the back of his head: for then the influx which is from the Lord is disturbed." Nor should we forget that entry in Emerson's *Journals* in which he noted that "for pure intellect" he had never known the equal of — Bronson Alcott!

It is true that these essays are not Emerson's best, but they were written when he was over forty years old and at the height of his fame and mental maturity, and they help us to understand our problem. They are typical products of the American mind. Conventional praise is given to the great names of Europe, with comment that indicates lack of understanding of the great currents of thought and action, while Mrs. Eddy and Brigham Young peer over the writer's shoulders. We begin to see how deeply Emerson was an American.

His national limitation is noteworthy in another important source of influence in a mature culture, that of art. Music appears to have been outside his life and consideration. Of painting he could write that, having once really seen a great picture, there was nothing for one to gain by looking at it again. In sculpture he finds a "paltriness, as of toys and the trumpery of a theater." It "is the game of a rude and youthful people, and not the manly labor of a wise and spiritual nation," and he quotes with approval Isaac Newton's remark about "stone dolls." Art is not mature unless it is "practical and moral," and addresses the uncultivated with a "voice of lofty cheer." All art should be extempore, and he utters a genuine American note in his belief that it will somehow come to us in a new form, the religious heart raising "to a divine use the railroad, the insurance office, the joint-stock company, our

law, our primary assemblies, our commerce, the galvanic battery, the electric jar, the prism, and the chemist's retort." "America is a poem in our eyes; its ample geography dazzles the imagination, and it will not wait long for metres." A century later, and we realize that something more is needful for the imagination than an ample geography.

His doctrine that art should be extempore stems from his general belief that knowledge comes from intuition rather than from thought, and that wisdom and goodness are implanted in us — a fatally easy philosophy which has always appealed to the democratic masses, and which is highly flattering to their self-esteem. Wordsworth had led the romantic reaction by making us see the beauty and value in the common things of everyday life, but the philosophy of Emerson has a different ancestry. The two when joined are a perfect soil for democratic belief, and democratic laxity in mind and spirit, far as that might be from Emerson's intention and occasional statements. The more obvious inferences are dangerous, for although a cobbler's flash of insight *may* be as great as the philosopher's lifetime of thought, such is of the rarest occurrence, and preached as a universal doctrine it is a more leveling one by far than universal suffrage.

2

As the ordinary unimportant man, such as most of us are, reads Emerson, his self-esteem begins to grow and glow. "The sweetest music is not in the oratorio, but in the human voice when it speaks from its instant tones of tenderness, truth, or courage." Culture, with us, he says, "ends in headache." "Do not craze yourself with thinking, but go about your business anywhere. Life is not intellectual or critical, but sturdy." "Why all this deference to Alfred and Scanderbeg and Gustavus? As great a stake depends on your private act to-day as followed their public and renowned steps." "We are all wise. The difference between persons is not in wisdom but in art." "Our spontaneous action is always the best. You cannot with your best deliberation and heed come so close to any question as your spontaneous glance shall bring you whilst you rise from your bed."

There is a kernel of noble thought in all this, but it is heady doctrine that may easily make men drunk and driveling, and I think we are coming near to the heart of our problem. The preaching that we do not have to think, the doctrine of what I may term, in Emerson's phrase, "the spontaneous glance," is at the bottom of that appalling refusal to criticize, analyze, ponder, which is one of the chief characteristics of the American people to-day in all its social, political, and international affairs. Many influences have united to bring about the condition, and Emerson cannot escape responsibility for being one of them.

On the other hand, a new nation, a common man with a fleeting vision of the possibility of an uncommon life, above all the youth just starting out with ambition and hope but little knowledge or influence as yet, all need the stimulation of a belief that somehow they *are* important and that not only may their private acts and lives be as high and noble as any, but that the way is open for them to make them so. This is the one fundamental American doctrine. It is the one unique contribution America has made to the common fund of civilization. Our mines and wheat fields do not differ in kind from others. With Yankee ingenuity we have seized on the ideas of others and in many cases improved their practical applications. The ideas, however, have largely come from abroad. The use of coal as fuel, the harnessing of steam and electricity for man's use, — the foundations of our era, — originated in Europe. Even the invention of the electric light was only in part American. But the doctrine of the importance of the common man is uniquely an American doctrine. It is something different, on the one hand, from the mere awarding to him of legal rights and, on the other, from the mere career open to the talents.

It is a doctrine to which the heart of humanity has responded with religious enthusiasm. It, and not science, has been the real religion of our time, and, essentially, the doctrine is a religious and not a philosophical or scientific one, equally made up as it is of a colossal hope and a colossal illusion. This does not invalidate it. Like all religions it will have its course to run and its part to play in the moulding of man to something finer. It is one more step up, and we need not deny it merely because of the inherent falsity of that gorgeous preamble which proclaims to the world, "All men are created equal." In spite of the self-assertion of the so-called masses, that is a statement which, deep in their hearts, it is as difficult for the inferior as the superior genuinely to believe. It is an ideal, which, like every religious ideal, will be of far-reaching influence, but which must be made believable emotionally. Emerson's greatness lies in his having been the greatest prophet of this new religion, an influence that might well continue to be felt on the two classes that need the doctrine most — the common man striving to rise above the mediocre, and the youth striving to attain a courageous and independent maturity.

Another strain in Emerson, that of the poet and mystic, has also to be reckoned with in making up the man's account.

His insistence upon values in life, culminating in the spiritual, is one sorely needed in the America of our day as of his. We are, perhaps, further from the ideal he drew in his "American Scholar" than were the men of his own time. His large hope has not been fulfilled. There is a delicate beauty in his spiritual outlook on life, a beauty akin to that of many an old fresco in Umbria or Tuscany. Unfortunately, there were fundamenal flaws in the work of the Italian artists, flaws not of spiritual insight or of artistic craftsmanship, but of wet plaster or of wrong chemical combinations in materials, so that little by little their painting has crumbled and faded. If Emerson's mysticism led him too easily toward Swedenborg rather than toward Plato, and if the beauty of his spiritual interpretation of the universe does not carry that conviction or mould his readers as it should, may we not wonder whether there were not some fundamental flaws in the mind of the man that may explain his decreasing influence, just as in examining a wall where a few patches of dim color are all that remain of a Giotto we have to consider, not the artist's love of the Madonna, but his lack of knowledge of the mechanics of his art? Of this we shall speak presently.

The quintessence of Emersonianism is to be found in the first and second series of *Essays,* and it may be noted that it was these, as my pencilings show, which I myself read most as a boy, and of them, it was such essays as "Self-Reliance," in which the word is found in its purest form, that I read over and over. What do I find marked as I turn the old pages? "Trust thyself: every heart vibrates to that iron string." "Whoso would be a man must be a nonconformist." "Nothing at last is sacred but the integrity of your own mind." "I do not wish to expiate, but to live. My life is not an apology, but a life. It is for itself and not for a spectacle." "What I must do is all that concerns me, not what the people think." "The great man is he who in the crowd keeps with perfect sweetness the independence of solitude." "Always scorn appearances and you always may. The force of character is cumulative." "Life only avails and not the having lived." "Insist on yourself; never imitate." "Nothing can bring you peace but yourself."

This is high and worthy doctrine, the practice of which will tax a man's strength and courage to the utmost, and such sentences as the above have proved the strongest influences in the making of literally countless adolescent Americans, stimulating their ambition in the noblest fashion. Unfortunately this part of Emerson's teaching has had less influence than the other. The average American soon slips into preferring "we are all wise" to "scorn appearances." Insisting on being one's self is strenuous and difficult work anywhere, more so in America than any other country I know, thanks to social opinion, mass ideals, and psychologized advertising of national products. Emerson deserves full meed of praise for preaching the value of individualism, but it may be asked, granting that nearly all intelligent, high-minded American youths for nearly a century have, at their most idealistic stage, come under the influence of Emerson's doctrine, why has the effect of his teaching been so slight upon their later manhood? Does the fault lie in them or in the great teacher, for, in such sentences as we have quoted above, I gladly allow that the sage of Concord *was* a great teacher.

The answer, I think, is that the fault lies to a great extent in Emerson himself. His doctrine contains two great flaws, one positive, the other negative, and both as typically American as he himself was in everything. That he had no logically articulated system of thought is not his weakest point. He once said that he could not give an account of himself if challenged. Attempts have been made to prove that his thought was unified and coherent. One may accept these or not. It matters little, for it is not, and never has been, as a consistent philosopher that Emerson has influenced his readers. It has been by his trenchant aphorisms which stir the soul of the young and the not too thoughtful, and set the blood to dancing like sudden strains of martial music. It is in these, and not in any metaphysical system about which philosophers might argue, that we find the fatal flaws and influences I have mentioned.

The first, the positive one, in spite of his high doctrine of self-reliance and individualism, is that Emerson makes life too easy by his insistence on intuition and spontaneity. The style and construction of his writings deliberately emphasize the import of the aphorisms. The occasionally qualifying context sinks into insignificance and out of memory as does the stick of a rocket in the darkness of night. We see and recall only the dazzling shower of stars. If this is now and then unfair to Emerson's thought, he has himself to blame. He took no pains to bind his thought together and loved the brilliancy of his rocket-stars of "sayings." We have already quoted some of these on the point we are now discussing. All teaching is "Intuition." In "Spontaneity or Instinct" he finds "the essence of genius, the essence of virtue, and the essence of life." "It is as easy for the strong man to be strong, as it is for the weak to be weak." "All good conversation, manners, and action, come from a spontaneity which forgets usages, and makes the moment great." "No man need be perplexed by his speculations. . . . These are the soul's mumps and measles and whooping-coughs." "Our moral nature is vitiated by any interference of our will. . . . There is no merit in the matter. Either God is there or he is not there. We love characters in proportion as they are impulsive and spontaneous. The less a man thinks or knows about his virtues the better we like him." A page or two back we noted his theory of spontaneity in art and intellect.

3

This, as we have said, unless the occasional qualifications are as greatly emphasized as the sayings themselves, is extremely dangerous doctrine. Of all the youths who have read Emerson in their impressionable years, a certain proportion have subsequently retrograded in the spiritual and intellectual scale, and a certain proportion have advanced. Of the difficulty with the master felt by the latter we shall speak presently, but for the first group this doctrine of spontaneity, so emphasized by Emerson, offers all too soft a cushion upon which to recline. Act and do not think. Culture is headache. Perplexities are the soul's mumps and measles. Radiant sentence after sentence, graven with clear precision on the cameo of the mind. It has been said that, of all the sages, Emerson requires the least intellectual preparation to read. He is, indeed, in some respects, and those in which he exerts most influence, fatally easy. Fatally easy and alluring to the busy hundred-per-cent American is this doctrine of intuition and spontaneity. It is a siren voice, a soft Lydian air blown across the blue water of the mind's tropical sea. For a century the American has left the plain hard work of life to his foreign serfs. The backbreaking toil of digging trenches, laying rails, puddling iron in the furnaces, has been delegated successively to the Irish, the Italians, the Slavs. But thinking is intellectually, willing is spiritually, as backbreaking as these. The ordinary American prefers also to abandon them and to take for himself the easier task of solving the economic problems and puzzles in which he delights. Intuition and spontaneity — fatal words for a civilization which is more and more coming to depend for its very existence on clear, hard, and long-sustained "thinking-through." It is this positive flaw in Emerson's teaching that has made the effect of his really noble doctrines of so little influence upon the boys who have worshiped him this side idolatry at sixteen and then gone into the world and found every invitation to retreat from the high ground rather than to advance.

What now of those others, those who also worshiped Emerson in youth, who have fought the world, and who find him declining in influence over their lives the more they advance? With them we reach Emerson's negative flaw.

What a gulf between the man of fifty and the boy of sixteen! As one has in those intervening years studied the history of the past, watched the daily life of the people of a score of nations, seen wars and famines take their toll of millions, and, nearer one's own heart, watched the physical pain of those closest to one's self, stood at grave after grave, found, too, perhaps, that one has wrought evil when most striving to do good, one has come to feel the whole mystery of that problem of Evil — of sin, of suffering, of death. One may yet carry a brave heart and hold one's self erect, but one is no longer content with a phi-losophy of shallow optimism, a "God's in his heaven — all's right with the world."

I think that here is where Emerson fails us as we grow older and wiser. The trumpet blasts of self-reliance which so thrilled us at sixteen sound a little thin and far-off now. We needed them when they first smote our ear and we are deeply grateful, but we have fought the fight, we have tried to be ourselves, we have tried to live our life for itself and not for a spectacle, and now we are older. We have lived, loved, suffered, enjoyed, fought, and to some extent won. The world has been rich in interest — and in suffering. There are hopeful signs on every side. There is sunlight as well as darkness, but there *is* darkness. One has been close to failure and looked it in the eye. There have been the brows we could not soothe through years of suffering, the waxen faces we kissed for the last time before we laid them away, the mysterious darkness coming toward ourselves like the shadow of a cloud on a summer landscape, but inevitably to overtake us. When we turn again to the great teacher of our youth, what does he say to help or hearten us? Nothing.

Owing largely to material circumstance and a vast and uninhabited continent, the prevailing mood of the American people came to be one of shallow and unlimited optimism, the waves of which flowed over even the sectional Calvinism of New England. Nature ceased to be the evil enemy of man's spirit and gave him her fairest gifts, as Mephistopheles bestowed his Helen on the tortured Faust. With material abundance, spiritual evil ceased to appear important and a golden age seemed dawning, as youth came to Faust in that most un-American legend.

For its hundred and fifty years America has been scarcely touched by suffering. Pestilence? None. Think of the Black Death and other great plagues that have swept over Europe. Famine? None. Think of India and China. War? Scarcely more than one. In the Revolution only an infinitesimal part of the population was in the army for any length of time. The War of 1812 was a ripple, almost all at sea, and the deaths were negligible to the population. The Indian Wars? Skirmishes by paid troops. The Mexican War? A junket which never came home to the people. The Civil War? Yes, but even that did not come home to the whole civilian population, except in the South, as have the wars which have flowed in torrents over Europe. Compare it with the Thirty Years' War, in which, to say nothing of the rest of Europe, the population of Germany, from the ravages of the sword, famine, disease, and emigration, sank from 16,000,000 to 6,000,000, and in which of 35,000 villages in Bohemia less than 6000 were standing at the end, and in which nine tenths of the entire population of the Palatinate disappeared. The Spanish War was a holiday affair except for a few homes. In the last Great War we lost by death a mere 126,000 as compared with 8,500,000 in the Old World. In civil life our history has been one long business boom, punctuated by an occasional panic, like a fit of indigestion for a man who continually overeats. We have never suffered like the rest of humanity, and have waxed fat without, as yet, having to consider the problems forced upon others, until we have ceased to believe in their reality. The dominant American note has thus been one of a buoyant and unthinking optimism. America is a child who has never gazed on the face of death.

Emerson somewhere speaks of "the nonchalance of boys sure of a dinner."

Can any words better express the American attitude toward the universe, and, in spite of his spirituality and the somewhat faded fresco of his mysticism, does Emerson himself really give us anything deeper? Man, according to him, "is born to be rich." Economic evils trouble our sage not at all. The universe, for him, is good through and through, and "success consists in close application to the laws of the world, and, since those laws are intellectual and moral, an intellectual and moral obedience." One thinks of Jay Gould and the career of many a magnate of to-day! "In a free and just commonwealth, property rushes from the idle and imbecile, to the industrious, brave, and persevering." As I am certainly not idle (I am working on a holiday to write this), and as Americans would not admit that theirs is not a just and free commonwealth, imbecility is the only third horn of the trilemma on which to impale myself if property has not rushed toward me. "Do not skulk," the sage tells every man in "a world which exists for him." At fifty, we have found, simply, that the world does *not* exist for us. "Love and you shall be loved. All love is mathematically just, as much as the two sides of an algebraic problem." One rubs one's eyes. "There is a soul at the center of nature and over the will of every man, so that none of us can wrong the universe." Man may, he says, "easily dismiss all particular uncertainties and fears, and adjourn to the sure revelation of time the solution of his private riddles. He is sure his welfare is dear to the heart of being." Is he so sure? Alas, no longer.

4

As I think over my most recent visit to Rome, where two thousand years of human history, happiness, and suffering have left their monuments, and Heaven knows how many thousand unmarked before, I contrast it with a visit to Emerson's house at Concord on an October day many years ago. It is a charming, roomy old house, and in it Emerson was able to live with a large library and three servants on two thousand a year. In the ineffable light of an American autumn, as I saw it, it was a place of infinite peace. Concord in 1840 was an idyllic moment in the history of the race. That moment came and passed, like a baby's smile. Emerson lived in it. "In the morning," he wrote, "I awake, and find the old world, wife, babies, and mother, Concord and Boston, the dear old spiritual world, and even the dear old devil not far off."

It is true that he has very occasional qualms and doubts. He even wonders in one essay whether we must presuppose some "slight treachery and derision" in the universe. As we turn the pages, we ask ourselves with some impatience, "Did this man never really suffer?" and read that "the only thing grief has taught me, is to know how shallow it is. That, like all the rest, plays about the surface, and never introduces me into the reality, for contact with which, we would even pay the costly price of sons and lovers."

One ends. Perhaps Mr. More is right. Perhaps Emerson *is* the outstanding figure in American letters. Who else has expressed so magnificently the hope, and so tragically illustrated the illusion, of our unique contribution to the world? My own debt to the sage is unpayable. He was one of the great influences in my early life, as, in his highest teaching, he should be in that of every boy. It seems almost the basest of treason to write this essay, and I would still have every youth read his Emerson. But what of America? What of the hope and the illusion? A century has passed. Is no one to arise

who will fuse them both in some larger synthesis, and who, inspiring youth, will not be a broken reed in maturity? Are our letters and philosophy to remain the child until the Gorgon faces of evil, disaster, and death freeze our own unlined ones into eternal stone? Is it well that the outstanding figure in American letters should be one whose influence diminishes in proportion as the minds of his readers grow in strength, breadth, and maturity? And, speaking generally, is this not true of Emerson? Does any man of steadily growing character, wealth of experience, and strength of mind find the significance and influence of Emerson for him growing as the years pass? Does he turn to him more and more for counsel, help, or solace?

There is but one answer, I think, and that is negative. Unlike the truly great, the influence of Emerson shrinks for most of us as we ourselves develop. May the cause not lie in the two flaws I have pointed out, flaws in the man as in his doctrine in spite of the serene nobility of so much of his life? If with all his wide and infinitely varied reading, noted in his *Journals*, we find his culture a bit thin and puerile, is it not because he himself trusted too much to that theory of spontaneity, of the "spontaneous glance," rather than to the harder processes of scholarship and thinking-through coherently; and if we find him lacking in depth and virility, is it not because he allowed himself to become a victim to that vast American optimism with its refusal to recognize and wrestle with the problem of evil? One turns to Æschylus and reads: —

. . . affliction knows no rest,
But rolls from breast to breast its vagrant tide.

One does not need to be a pessimist,

merely human, to find here the deeper and more authentic note.

If Emerson is still the outstanding figure in American letters, is that not the equivalent of saying that America a century after the *Essays* appeared has not yet grown to mental maturity, and that the gospel it preaches is inspiring only for unformed adolescence, — of whatever age, — without having risen to a comprehension of the problems of maturity? In Europe, the past has bequeathed not only a wealth of art, but a legacy of evil borne and sorrow felt. Perhaps American letters, like American men, will not grow beyond the simple optimism and, in one aspect, the shallow doctrine of Emerson until they too shall have suffered and sorrowed. Emerson, in his weakness as in his strength, is American through and through. He could have been the product, in his entirety, of no other land, and that land will not outgrow him until it has some day passed through the fires of a suffering unfelt by him and as yet escaped by it.

Stuart Gerry Brown: EMERSON, 1803-1953

Stuart Gerry Brown is Professor of American Studies at the University of Hawaii. Among his books are: Conscience in Politics: Adlai E. Stevenson in the 1950's; Thomas Jefferson; *and* The American Presidency: Leadership, Partisanship, and Popularity.

This essay is a direct reply to J. T. Adams. Professor Brown agrees that there is a utopian anarchistic strain in Emerson's thought, which — taken literally — would justify Adams's strictures. But to do so is to forget that Emerson is a poet and to substitute for the whole man "a pastiche of quotations wrenched from the context." Emerson recognized the necessity of parties and the conflicts of interest upon which they are founded; yet there is need also for those who by standing apart may the better appeal to the consciences of individuals. This role Emerson fulfilled until the great juncture of resistance, the Compromise of 1850, forced him to become an agitator for a cause. Democracy as a moral principle transcends the rights of a majority. If a law, the Fugitive Slave Act, is patently immoral, then it must not be obeyed. Emerson's individualism is not the expression of an adolescent revolt against conformity, but of the conviction that only through an appeal to everyone's conscience can parties and institutions be reformed.

WHEN he reread Emerson twenty years ago, James Truslow Adams found the Sage of Concord useful, even inspiring, for a boy of seventeen, but dull for a grown man. Emerson, it seemed to him, was the proper sign of America's boyhood, indeed had lived in it, and only delayed adolescence could account for

Reprinted from *Ethics*, "Emerson: 1803–1953" by Stuart Gerry Brown, pp. 217–25, by permission of The University of Chicago Press and of the author. Copyright 1954 by The University of Chicago.

his continued popularity. If, as Paul Elmer More put it, Emerson was, by both national and international standards, the outstanding American man of letters, Adams could only conclude that America had not yet outgrown its childish enthusiasm for the naïve and the visionary. Some day when Americans had "passed through the fires of a suffering unfelt by him [Emerson]," they would cast him off and find at last, presumably, an adult spokesman.

I

This was in 1930. Three years later, on the fourth day of March, Americans, many of whom were indeed really suffering, heard with eager and pathetic attention the voice of a mature man speaking "their own rejected thoughts":

So first of all let me assert my firm belief that the only thing we have to fear is fear itself. . . . Stripped of the lure of profit by which to induce our people to follow their false leadership, they [the money changers] have resorted to exhortations, pleading tearfully for restored confidence. They know only the rules of a generation of self-seekers.

They have no vision, and when there is no vision the people perish.

The money changers have fled from their high seats in the temple of our civilization. We may now restore that temple to the ancient truths.

In the ensuing years that voice spoke with ever greater firmness and confidence for ever more people, until by 1941 it was voicing the maturing aspiration of the free people of the whole world. The minimum needs for a world which had suffered such "fires of torment" as men had never known before were, he said, four freedoms, of which the last and most urgent was "freedom from fear."

A hundred years ago, in the "child-hood" of America, Emerson lectured his fellow citizens as they cowered before the awful fact that the slavery issue could no longer be comfortably avoided:

We never get beyond our first lesson, for, really, the world exists, as I understand it, to teach the science of liberty, which begins with liberty from fear. . . . There is no help but in the head and heart and hamstrings of a man . . . he only who is able to stand alone is qualified for society. . . . Why have the minority no influence? Because they have not a real minority of one.

No one supposes that Franklin Roosevelt searched in Emerson for his text. He had no need to search there or elsewhere in books. He found in his own heart and in the hearts of his countrymen, as Emerson foretold, the word the times called for. He found it and he spoke it, simply and forthrightly. This is what Emerson himself had done in the gray years before the Civil War. It is no accident that the words spoken should have been so nearly identical. At each moment of public crisis and popular despair the urgent call is the same. To see this we but need be reminded, again and again, that we are men, that fear is of our own fabrication and making, that he who fears to rely upon himself is no reliable force in collective action and organization. The plain truth is that Emerson spoke out of a fullness and maturity of human understanding seldom achieved by public men. But like the wisest professors of the university, who are commonly the most scoffed at and misunderstood by sophomores, he could only seem dull and impractical to our most sophomoric generation — that which immediately followed the first World War. What is unfortunate is that we who have vital use for Emerson have been nourished and diverted by the teachings and interpretations of that generation. He has become for us, under such auspices, the hopelessly impractical preacher of an individualism so extreme that the world has long since passed him by, if, indeed, it ever could conveniently have contained him. He gives us, it appeared to James Truslow Adams, nothing better than "the nonchalance of boys sure of a dinner."

Now there is, admittedly, a certain basis for this claim. The immediate practical application, for example, of Emerson's doctrine of nonconformity would surely produce unbounded chaos, and lay us open to devastating attack, both moral and physical, from the disciplined forces of totalitarianism. And his doctrines of inconsistency and pure self-reliance are hardly calculated to solve the problems of economic security or world peace. Taken at random or taken piecemeal, Emerson is certainly a vintner of heady wines, and the world has, no doubt, rather more need of sober sense than of drunken abandon.

But in all truth such is not the Emerson who so stirred the hearts of Americans, from the time of Jackson to the Civil War. This Emerson of fiction is not, in fact, a real man at all, but a pastiche of quotations wrenched from the context, not only of the pages on which they were written but of the age to which they belong. If we restore that context, we shall find the real Emerson, a prophet whose value for Americans of 1953 is perhaps not less than it was for his contemporaries.

II

In the summer of 1832, when he was twenty-nine, a long struggle in Emerson's conscience came to a climax. Partly, no doubt, because of a mood of despondency after losing his beloved wife, Ellen Tucker, but principally because he could not reconcile the mission of the spiritual leader with even the pale shadow of the priest of ritual, he broke finally with his congregation of the Second Church in Boston and retired from public life. He turned his back on the God of the market place to face the God of the Universe. The Emerson of the essays, poems, and lectures, the Emerson with whom the world is familiar, shows little sign of an early career in the Christian ministry. In those writings, indeed, Jesus appears infrequently and then usually as one of several in a catalogue of spiritual and religious teachers. Actually Emerson seems to have drawn more freely and more comfortably upon the religious wisdom of the Orient than upon the tradition to which he belonged. Yet a glance at the correspondence and journals of his early years shows that he had always been intended, and intended himself, for the ministry. Careful second glance will show why. With the earliest entries one finds indications of radicalism and rebellion. At Harvard as an undergraduate he was drawn but little to the Unitarian divines among the faculty and visiting lecturers. Courses in orthodox Christian morality and theology left him cold. Instead he invested his time in unguided studies of the pre-Christian Greeks and of the English poets. When, in a brief career of school teaching, he had saved sufficient money to enter divinity school, his correspondence with his remarkable Aunt Mary shows that he chose Harvard precisely because it was the least orthodox school in New England, sharply against the wishes of those who recommended Brown for the purity of its theology. Even as he entered the Divinity School in 1821 he was already in more or less conscious revolt against the Christian ministry and the Christian church. But his desire to contribute to the elevation of popular morality, to assert effectively the dignity and sweetness of the individual man, could find, it seemed to him, its best opportunity in the pulpit. His calling was to be a prophet, not a priest.

His young career as a churchman was promising. Before he was thirty his reputation for pulpit oratory extended broadly over eastern New England, and his election to the pastorship of the Second Church was an honor as befitting as it was signal. In many ways the Unitarianism of Channing which prevailed in Emerson's time was radical enough and unorthodox enough. The Unitarian preacher was indeed free to say almost whatever he pleased. But there were vestiges of the priestly function. The Lord's Supper had to be commemorated, though belief in its miraculous benefits, as well as the supernatural metaphysics upon which it rested, had long since been discarded. Emerson became restive in ministering to a congregation which could hear him with applause while he directed his exhortations toward individual self-betterment and expounded the gospels in human and secular terms, yet still felt a need for dramatization of what seemed to him outworn superstition. He put it to them frankly; his congregation as frankly replied; and they parted company. He had already reached what they had not yet glimpsed — the wisdom of Santayana's subsequent discernment that "religion is poetry which is mistaken for science."

He went to Europe, and especially to England, to take there the measure of those living men of thought who had helped him to make a radical reappraisal of religion, morals, and politics. He found them all wanting. Landor was brilliant but superficial; Coleridge was confused and vacillating; Wordsworth had become a complacent Tory; only Carlyle struck him as an original character. But in spite of the immediate and lifelong friendship recorded in their brilliant correspondence, Emerson never became Carlyle's disciple. Their resemblances are of the surface only; below lies the difference between Calvin and Jefferson. But if the European trip was a disappointment, it was also a great source of inspiration. What the leaders in the Old World had seemed to do but had not done could be freshly attempted in the New.

Greatness appeals to the future. If I can be firm enough today to do right, and scorn eyes, I must have done so much right before as to defend me now. Be it how it will, do right now. . . . Where is the master who could have taught Shakespeare? Where is the master who could have instructed Franklin, or Washington, or Bacon, or Newton?

And so he returned to Boston, and presently to Concord, to take up his calling once more, this time beyond the cloisters, for all time in the broad fields of the world. The need for his spiritual mission was real. It was 1834, and Andrew Jackson was fighting Nicholas Biddle over the Bank of the United States. The first great hue and cry was being raised against Wall Street and Broad Street. Permanent party lines of America were being formed. The Whigs were learning how to organize for the defense of vested property and financial interest. The Democrats were massing their energies to check and destroy the power of the Whigs. It was a moment of high political tension. But within the parties, there was a deadly conformity. The Whig must be wary lest a moment of enthusiasm betray him into an expression of unorthodoxy that would undermine his reputation as a sound and conservative citizen. Let the Democrat equally beware lest there arise a taint of suspicion that he could not be counted on in the party caucus. The guardians of Whiggery and of Democracy alike kept their minions well in line. On one conformity both parties were agreed — to look away from the dark shadow of human slavery. It was this age of which the young French diplomat de Tocqueville said, "Freedom of opinion does not exist in America," and Harriet Martineau, that ". . . the subservience to opinion at that time seemed a sort of mania." John Jay Chapman writing in 1898 described it in these words:

The South was a plantation. The North crooked the hinges of the knee where thrift might follow fawning. It was the era of Martin Chuzzlewit, a malicious caricature — founded on fact. This time of humiliation, when there was no free speech, no literature, little manliness, no reality, no simplicity, no accomplishment, was the era of American brag. We flattered the foreigner and we boasted of ourselves. We were over-sensitive, insolent, and cringing.

Because he saw the mediocrity and felt the fear in his age, and because he knew that the mediocrity and the fear were at bottom the same thing, Emerson saw his own mission as needing to be carried out on a plane above the conflict of parties. The overwhelming merit of democracy lay then, as now, in its offering to all men a fair opportunity for self-realization, for creative growth in freedom under law, for achieving the resolution of differences in peace. But the process of democracy assumes that the freedoms it guarantees and the opportunities it offers will be taken up by men, and exercised. The whole case for democracy depends upon the character of the individuals who practice it. Emerson saw greater danger in the mediocrity and the fear than in either the banks or the spoils system. For twenty years his mighty service to his country was to preach the curative gospel of self-reliance.

In such a context the doctrine of nonconformity can be seen in its true perspective. "Whoso would be a man must be a non-conformist. . . . I would write on the lintels of the door-post, *Whim*" — as against the discipline of party mediocrity or the closed corporation of finance.

We must hold a man amenable to reason for the choice of his daily craft or profession. It is not an excuse any longer for his deeds, they are the custom of his trade. What business has he with an evil trade? Has he not a *calling* in his character?

As he said repeatedly in his lectures up and down the land, Emerson saw a necessity for both the Conservative and Radical parties in the world, but the division between them must be based on the "considerate vote of single men spoken on their honor and their conscience." This was the *must* of democracy. The reality was the self-seeking of persons drawn together into organizations for the sake of self-seeking. Conservatism and radicalism were principles in the nature of man and of society, and parties must reflect them as principles. The reality was a division of interests. Emerson knew well enough that when he preached self-reliance, derived from the classic idealism of Greece, to an audience of frontiersmen and settlers thirsting for culture, he was risking a cheap success owed to misunderstanding. Self-reliance, of a sort, was assuredly the practice in the new West and no vague ideal of

moral betterment. And it was precisely
Emerson's genius that he could seize hold
of that practice and show its potentiality,
by reinterpretation, for the reconstruction of the moral life. The proof lay in
his repeated invitations to return. Between 1835 and 1850 he travelled thousands of miles and visited and revisited
hundreds of cities and towns. His largest
return for a year of speaking was little
more than $2,000. It was hard work,
and the real rewards were intangible.
But it was the work of a man. Without
it the spiritual leadership of Lincoln,
when it came, might well have had a
smaller following.

It was a work Emerson could not have
carried on had he been a joiner. The
radical appeal of his public talk brought
him innumerable pleas and pressures to
aid in this reform or lead in that movement. Not a few reforms were in fact
inspired by his teaching, and it brought
him genuine distress that he felt himself
obliged to say no. It has always been an
easy criticism of Emerson that he kept
aloof from practical affairs and so did
not run the risk of criticism and satire his
followers accepted. But he hewed to his
course, as one who knew what he was
doing. Had he allowed his energies to
be dissipated in the agitations of the
reformers — even the Abolitionists — his
unique influence would have been lost.
And in his heart he knew that the reform
of parties and institutions succeeds only
when it moves with the reform of individuals.

Nature will not have us fret and fume. She
does not like our benevolence or our learning
much better than she likes our frauds and
wars. When we come out of the caucus, or
the bank, or the Abolition-convention, or the
Temperance-meeting, or the Transcendental
club, into the fields and woods, she says to
us, "So hot? my little sir."

III

When the early Abolitionists urged
Emerson to join their ranks, his reply
was, "I have my own spirits in prison; —
spirits in deeper prisons, whom no man
visits if I do not." He put it thus largely
because it was a good part of the truth,
but also because the mission we have
been describing was not easy for him to
explain without a suspicion of arrogance.
It is also true that he was repelled by the
personality of men like Garrison. He
feared and detested fanaticism, even in
a good cause. Though he did not predict,
he might well have predicted, on his
own philosophy, that Garrison would one
day publicly burn the Constitution of
the United States. The cause of enlightenment in America, the cultivation
of the moral life, was not to be advanced
by such measures. Yet through all the
years he felt deeply that human slavery
transcended all other practical issues of
the day and laid a curse and a blight
upon the American democracy. He
hoped that the belief in human dignity
could be so spread about the land that
in the end Americans would out of shame
abolish the institution of slavery. Though
more frequently than not he cast his vote
with the Democratic party and thought
it proper that intellectual men should do
so, in the matter of slavery he accepted
the leadership of Daniel Webster, for
whom his admiration was in any case
very great.

But his very aloofness from politics
kept him in considerable ignorance of
the actual character of public men, including Webster. That Webster was the
appointed and adaptable spokesman of
economic privilege and power, Emerson
seems not for many seasons to have realized. He was at first envious of Webster's
oratorical skill and was beguiled by the
golden periods of high sounding oratory.

And so he was shocked by the Compromise of 1850, the Fugitive Slave Law, and, above all, by Webster's 7th of March speech. But if he was not prepared for the personal defection of Webster, he was perhaps better prepared than any other American for the occasion itself. He might have been speaking of himself when he told an audience in Concord:

There are men who are as sure indexes of the equity of legislation and of the same state of public feeling, as the barometer is of the weight of the air, and it is a bad sign when these are discontented, for though they snuff oppression and dishonor at a distance, it is because they are more impressionable: the whole population will in a short time be as painfully affected.

The time had come, in 1850, when all the years should bear their fruit. The great generalizations of freedom, dignity, individual self-reliance, nonconformity, and forthright speech had now an issue worthy of their application by any man. The compromise of slavery at the North itself called for the concerted action of all those precious individuals whom Emerson had all the while been trying to "draw out of the masses." It was a time for politics at last. Webster seemed to have laid down the gauntlet, and Emerson, inexperienced as he was in the discussion of public affairs, was yet better equipped than any other to take it up. He did so with quickness and decision.

The last year had forced us all into politics, and made it a paramount duty to seek what it is often a duty to shun. We do not breathe well. There is infamy in the air. I have a new experience. I wake in the morning with a painful sensation, which I carry about all day, and which, when traced home, is the odious remembrance of that ignominy which has fallen on Massachusetts, which robs the landscape of beauty, and takes the sunshine out of every hour.

Emerson, entering the lists with Webster, was, as Chapman described him, a magnificent fighting animal. The role of the agitator, he soon discovered, commanded far less respect than that of lecturer on culture, but he did not flinch when rowdy audiences in New York and elsewhere threw at him the adverse bouquets of eggs and tomatoes. He stood his ground and won his listeners by the evident sincerity of his conviction. He was content with no peripheral thrusts. Everything he said, denouncing the Fugitive Slave Law, attacking the principle of compromise with evil, and castigating the personal character of Webster, was aimed at the heart of the matter.

Mr. Webster tells the President that "he has been in the North, and he has found no man, whose opinion is of any weight, who is opposed to the law." Oh, Mr. President, trust not the information! The gravid old Universe goes spawning on; the womb conceives and the breasts give suck to thousands and millions of hairy babes formed not in the image of your statute, but in the image of the Universe; too many to be bought off; too many than they can be rich, and therefore peaceable; and necessitated to express first or last every feeling of the heart. You can keep no secret, for whatever is true some of them will unreasonably say. You can commit no crime, for they are created in their sentiments conscious of and hostile to it; and unless you can suppress the newspaper, pass a law against book-shops, gag the English tongue in America, all short of this is futile. This dreadful English Speech is saturated with songs, proverbs and speeches that flatly contradict and defy every line of Mr. Mason's statute. Nay, unless you can draw a sponge over those seditious Ten Commandments which are the root of our European and American civilization;

and over that eleventh commandment, "Do unto others as you would have them do to you," your labor is vain.

So much for the attempt to suppress truth. Compromise, he thought, is legitimate when it is compromise of the temporal, but beware of compromise with the eternal. Webster he found at last was no true democrat, no believer in the efficacy of popular government. So long as the commercial party could dominate behind the scenes, democratic oratory was safe enough, but when the curtain was pulled, as the Fugitive Slave Law pulled it, and the naked truth exposed, Webster was seen in his proper place.

Happily he was born late, — after the independence had been declared, the Union agreed to, and the constitution settled. What he finds already written, he will defend. Lucky that so much had got well written when he came. For he has no faith in the power of self-government; .... In Massachusetts, in 1776, he would, beyond all question, have been a refugee. ... So with the eulogies of liberty in his writings, — they are sentimentalism and youthful rhetoric.

There is not only earnest moral indignation in such passages as these, but also the bitterness of belated discovery. Emerson is personally aroused, and, as he would himself have been the first to confess, it is the personal element in public affairs which alone can draw the contemplative philosopher into action. Emerson's assumption of the role of agitator was implicit in all his life and teaching, but it took a personal reaction to Webster's defection to bring him into the fight, indeed to justify fighting at all. Webster's support of the Compromise of 1850 was personal. The real meaning of issues is always personal. Emerson's endless insistence that it is men who count

was now proved for him in immediate experience.

But if the Slave Law had brought about a situation in which the democrat could find no further room for compromise, what of the Union which the democratic process was intended to sustain? If democracy had reached the point at which it must fight or perish, what of the institutions of government which it had so painstakingly constructed over the long years since 1776?

I suppose the Union can be left to take care of itself. As much real union as there is, the statutes will be sure to express; as much disunion as there is, no statute can long conceal. Under the Union I suppose the fact to be that there are really two nations, the North and the South. It is not slavery that severs them, it is climate and temperament. The South does not like the North, slavery or no slavery, and never did. The North likes the South well enough, for it knows its own advantages. I am willing to leave them to the facts. If they continue to have a binding interest, they will be pretty sure to find it out: if not, they will consult their peace in parting. But one thing appears certain to me, that, as soon as the constitution ordains an immoral law, it ordains disunion. The law is suicidal, and cannot be obeyed. The Union is at an end as soon as an immoral law is enacted. And he who writes a crime into the statute-book digs under the foundations of the Capital to plant there a powder-magazine, and lays a train.

"Suicidal" is the key to this pronouncement. This is the ultimate limit of democracy. Compromise has touched bottom in the uncompromisable. The beauty and practical efficacy of the democratic process is that it can accommodate through compromise even extreme differences of attitude and principles. There are no conflicting programs for the development or modification of society which cannot be adjusted by democratic means, save only a program which envisions the destruction of democracy itself. The Compromise of 1850 was, therefore, no true compromise, since, by accepting the permanence of slavery in some parts of the Union and responsibility for it by all citizens, it proposed to withhold the liberties of free government from large numbers of the governed, and to do so under law. Not only the Union but democracy is at an end so soon as an immoral law is enacted, for an immoral law implies the contradiction of the process by which it is enacted.

Yet Emerson did not, even in 1851, call for a war to abolish slavery. In the proper spirit of liberty and democracy, he proposed still further attempts at peaceful solution: the rapid colonization of African territories by freed American Negroes; or the gradual emancipation of the slaves by the slave states in accordance with a policy developed by themselves; or emancipation at the expense of the taxpayers of the whole country with full remuneration to the owners, though their proprietorship would not be legally recognized. Anything and everything that offered even the smallest hope of success must be tried. That emancipation would one day come seemed to him as certain as the sunrise — that it should come peacefully was the test to which he and his countrymen were put. But if emancipation could not be achieved without violence, then the moral conscience of mankind, expressed through the civil freedoms of democracy, would know the ground upon which it must stand and fight. A Union without democracy was not worth having, and a Union with the institution of slavery made permanent by the false and odious compromise was a Union without democracy.

If there were moral weaklings and cowards upon whom the Websters of the government could count, then the mission of men like Emerson was clear. The conscience of such drifters and hypocrites must be aroused. The full meaning of the Fugitive Slave Law must be made plain to all mankind. Because the law was immoral and contradicted the principle upon which all law is sanctioned, it must be disobeyed. It would be necessary to condone extreme acts, even to speak on behalf of John Brown. If one could not follow Garrison in the public burning of the Constitution, one had nonetheless the evident duty to show how the Constitution was put to shame by the frightened law makers.

As one sees Emerson saying these things to all who would listen, in meetings public and private wherever he could conveniently go, one discerns with revealing clarity that all along he had been doing the work of democracy. From the plea for frankness and originality in "The American Scholar" and the denunciation of clerical pretense and hypocrisy in the "Divinity School Address" to the campaign against compromise grown cowardly and against human slavery twenty years later, there is a straight and ever clearer path.

In the attacks on Webster and the speeches on the Fugitive Slave Law, Emerson was saying nothing that had not been implicit from the beginning of his public career. He had not joined with the Jacksonians in their struggle to broaden the base of the suffrage, to free the people from the stranglehold of concentrated financial power, and to adjust the balance as between farmer and businessman, but he had nonetheless been a moral force for democracy, and he had remained uncompromised. When the split on the crucial issue of slavery brought disaster to the Democratic party — a disaster from which it would not recover for two generations — he bore no share of the responsibility. Because he did not join the Abolitionists, though he sympathized with their cause, he kept himself free of fanaticism, and so when the hour came he could speak without fear in the name of that democracy which the compromisers and the extremists had alike undermined. It was not Jackson or Garrison but Emerson who, as Chapman put it, sent ten thousand sons to the war.

IV

Viewed thus in the context of his own day, Emerson's maturity can scarcely be called into question. Those who depreciate him depreciate themselves. If his individualism has seemed visionary and boyish, it is because we have viewed it from one angle only and because our vision has been obscured by the intervening years. Like other great men of letters with a gift for style, Emerson has suffered because he is quotable. The aphorisms are too easily remembered, their purpose too easily forgotten. In our own time there is little danger that we shall adopt a philosophy of extreme individualism. The complexity of governmental and private organizations has developed and is continuing to develop in fair proportion to the complexity of the life we live. No one supposes that the unaided individual can now be the final force in public affairs. A hundred years ago Emerson saw that the moral purpose of Henry Thoreau could not justify his means, and, indeed, that the means themselves were impractical. So much the less is mere individual protest the order of our day.

Our danger lies rather in the other direction — that we shall rely too greatly on collective means for the achievement of the highest ends. The ever growing necessity for organization is leading us to ever greater dependence on the *idea* of organization. Because we cannot any longer divorce the individual from the groups of which he is a part, not wholly even in theory, we are risking the very existence of the individual as the constitutive element of democracy. Government by the people must be, no doubt, in practice government by organizations, and the organizations which by their interplay do the governing must themselves be composed of other organizations. But however the courts may have decided in the public law that a corporation is an individual, we dare not reduce this legal fiction to its logical absurdity — namely, that an organization is a man, or that man is wholly fulfilled in organization. Manliness is not a function of dependence, even a necessary dependence upon organization. The moral values of the purposes for which organizations exist and the human dignity of the means employed for their realization reflect as accurately in this day as in any other the character of the individuals who compose them. As in the 1850's Emerson could show his fellow citizens the exact proportion which healthy democracy bears to healthy men, that spurious compromise is the product of political cowardice, so in the 1950's he can show again what is the core of the American experience — that the issue is not big government and the welfare state against free enterprise and self-respect, nor public versus private techniques of economic management, but to promote the general welfare, by whatever measures the people agree upon, through the democratic process. He can show that the general welfare means not the welfare of organizations but the welfare of persons, that to confuse organizations, which are the legitimate means of democratic government, with the ends for which democratic government is maintained is to lose sight of the whole purpose of liberty. As free organization is the only valid answer to totalitarian regimenta-tion, it is the whole burden of Emerson's teaching and the meaning of his age that free organization requires free individuals.

"He only who is able to stand alone is qualified for society."

Henry Steele Commager: THEODORE PARKER

Henry Steele Commager, a leading American historian, now teaches at Amherst College. Of his many books the first is his distinguished biography of Theodore Parker.

Emerson was forced eventually into political activity, but to Parker agitation for reform — all sorts of reforms — came as naturally as breathing. There is no need, he felt, to be above the battle, since politics is applied morality. Parker, unlike Emerson, could then remain a preacher and be a partisan as well. He could align himself with the angels of light by becoming "father-confessor and spiritual advisor to all the leaders of the Free Soil and Republican Parties." Emerson tried to express the aspirations of Americans; Parker became "the Conscience of a Party." Was there some difficulty here? Professor Commager says: "A political realist, he saw the economic bases of politics; an idealist, he refused to recognize them or to accommodate himself to them." What sort of conscience was it that to avoid compromise spurred us on the way to civil war?

WHAT is a man born for, but to be a reformer. So Emerson had said, and was startled when they took him at his word. Every institution was called before the bar of reason, and of senti-ment — the Church, the State, labor, slavery, law and punishment, war, the school, the press, the family. Nothing was taken for granted, nothing but the right of inquiry and the authority of conscience. It was downright uncom-fortable to live in Boston in the forties and the fifties; it was not enough that you paid for your pew and stood well in State Street and sent your boys to Har-vard College; someone was sure to tell you that the Church was rotten and State Street wicked and that Harvard College taught nothing that a good man need know. Wherever you went the reformers demanded your credentials and your passport, and challenged every signature but their own. Even your private life was not immune; you could not eat or

From *Theodore Parker, Yankee Reformer,* by Henry Steele Commager, copyright 1936 by Little, Brown and Company. Reprinted by permission of the author. This extract comprises parts of Chapters 8 and 12.

drink in peace but someone would bob up to warn you that to touch meat was a vice and to sip wine a sin.

For the reformers, at least, Boston was the Hub of the Universe. Every town in New England sent its delegate there; they filled the halls with their conventions and the air with their clamor. There was an Aristides at every court, a Diogenes in every countinghouse. Here in this city of the Appletons and the Lees there were as many reformers as there were merchants. Call the roll of the radicals and their names crack out like a volley of musketry: Phillips, Sumner, Garrison, Mann, Quincy, Parker, Pierpont, Channing, Emerson, Alcott, Ripley, Loring, Lowell, Rantoul, Higginson, Howe. No mere fanatics these, no half-baked bedlamites; you could not dismiss a Quincy or a Channing or a Higginson, they were connected with half the families of the State. They could preach pantheism in the pulpit, transcendentalism in the schoolroom, socialism in the market place, abolitionism in Faneuil Hall; they could agitate the most inflammatory of issues, announce the most outlandish ideas, champion the most extravagant causes, and you would have to listen to them. And they consorted with the worst of men, and of women too. Wherever they went they trailed behind them clouds of high-flying enthusiasts — spiritualists, phrenologists, Swedenborgians, Millerites, vegetarians, Grahamites, prohibitionists, feminists, non-resistants, Thomsonians, Come-outers of every shape and every hue.

What had they in common, these reformers, men and women, rich and poor, educated and illiterate? What was it that persuaded Edmund Quincy to preside over the Chardon Street Convention and gave Channing patience to listen to the rantings of Abby Folsom and Sylvanus Brown? What was it that sent Parker and Ripley hot-footing it out to Groton to participate in the wrangling of the Millerites and the Come-outers? What was the magic of Brook Farm that it stirred the hearts of the sanest of men and made them tolerant even of Fruitlands and of Hopedale? Bronson Alcott had made a failure of everything but life, but no matter how fantastic his notions everyone loved him, for he had proved the Dignity of Man. Margaret Fuller was as dangerous as Fanny Wright, but all the women of Boston flocked to her Conversations, and Emerson was glad to contribute to her biography. Horace Mann succumbed to phrenology and Thomas Appleton flirted with spiritualism; Parker was fascinated by mesmerism and Emerson avowed himself a Swedenborgian and took lessons from Sampson Reed. Josiah Quincy thought well of the Mormons and admired Joseph Smith, and Ellis Gray Loring circulated petitions on behalf of Abner Kneeland, who was a convicted atheist and a Thomsonian too. Francis Jackson gave refuge to female abolitionists, Higginson hobnobbed with Lucy Stone and Amelia Bloomer, and Phillips championed the Woman's Movement as the greatest reform in history. Orestes Brownson founded a Society for Christian Progress, Robert Rantoul labored with Seth Parker for the ten-hour day, and John Allen of Brook Farm organized a New England Workingmen's Association, while Channing preached socialism from the pulpit and Parker congratulated the Shakers that they alone had solved the problem of industrialism. Charles Sumner enlisted with Garrison and Elihu Burritt in the war against war, and William Ladd projected a plan for a World Congress of Nations. Pierpont worked for temperance and Neal Dow

for prohibition; wealthy Reverend John
Sargent and poor John Augustus tried to
stamp out prostitution; Dorothea Dix
forced legislatures to ameliorate the lot
of the insane, and Samuel Gridley Howe
gave light to the blind. Phillips spoke
for penal reform and Parker described
the criminal as the victim, not the foe,
of society, and James Russell Lowell re-
buked the aged Wordsworth for his
defense of capital punishment: —

And always 'tis the saddest sight to see
An old man faithless in Humanity.

What had they in common — what but
a belief in the perfectibility of man and in
the doctrine of progress? Emerson had
put it well, Emerson who spoke for them,
however reluctantly:—"The power which
is at once spring and regulator in all
efforts of reform is the conclusion that
there is an infinite worthiness in man,
which will appear at the call of worth,
and that all particular reforms are the
removing of some impediment." They
were all transcendentalists, though they
read not Coleridge and knew not Kant.
They were all idealists, howsoever they
rationalized their emotions or tested
them by experience. The ability of man
to attain divinity, that was the point of
departure. It was assumption, as Rousseau's "Man is born free and is everywhere in chains" was an assumption —
as magnificent, as revolutionary in its
logical consequences. For if Man is a
God, how is it we find him a brute? If
man was born free, how is it we find
him in spiritual chains? The Calvinists
met this issue squarely enough: they rejected the assumptions. But transcendentalists took no stock in Original Sin
or the downfall of Man. They knew that
men were born not only free but to the
pursuit of happiness, and no matter how

sharply Mr. Garrison and Mr. Phillips
might take issue with Mr. Parker's theology, they too were transcendentalists at
heart.

No need to go to Saint Augustine for
the city of God — nor to Fourier, either.
No need to escape from reality into the
past, or to disown the present and go off
by yourself to some Brook Farm or
Walden Pond. What better place to build
the Heavenly City than here in Boston?
And what if the spirit of Hunkerism
ruled the town? What if dogma was
preached from the pulpits and servility
taught in the schools, and one third of
the people were from County Cork and
went to Mass? What if the merchants
built their proud houses on Beacon Hill
while the slums grew apace in South
Boston and the salt tide flooded the
cellars of the ramshackle tenements,
bringing disease and death? What if
there was a grog shop on every corner
and Deer Island was crowded with
wretched harlots; what if the law made
criminals and then killed them, and
Negroes were hunted in the streets of
Boston and sent back to the cotton fields
of the South? These things did not
prove the depravity of Man, for you
could not prove an untruth. You could
not invalidate a Natural Law by refusing to obey it.

That law was the Law of Progress.
Nature and Philosophy united to prove
the progress of mankind. Science (not
Professor Agassiz's) lent its support, and
even history — if you but read it aright
— even history demonstrated the sure
advance of civilization and the triumph
of right over wrong. Theirs was no easy
optimism, not the optimism that shaded
dangerously into a smug assurance that
whatever was, was right, nor yet an optimism so supremely confident of the
wisdom of Providence that it faltered

into fatalism. But they read with approval those lines from Locksley Hall —

Yet I doubt not through the ages one increasing purpose runs,
And the thoughts of men are widened with the process of the suns

and felt themselves in tune with the Infinite.

This is what gave them fortitude, the conviction that they were on the side of the angels, that they were fulfilling Nature and Nature's laws, and that the stars in their courses fought for them. This is what gave dignity to their zeal and strength to their numbers. It made them courageous in the face of opposition, resolute in the face of discouragement, eloquent in the face of apathy. It armored them against attack and fortified them against contumely. It gave them a militant, an unconquerable faith, that was at last triumphantly proclaimed by one who knew them all: —

He has sounded forth the trumpet that shall never call retreat;
He is sifting out the hearts of men before His judgment-seat;
O, be swift, my soul, to answer Him! be jubilant, my feet!
Our God is marching on.

God was marching on, but the Church lagged behind. It was, thought Parker, the most conservative of institutions, more concerned with ritual and with dogma than with life. No need to look to the Church for inspiration or support; "even the baby-virtue of America," wrote Parker contemptuously, "turns off from that lean, haggard and empty breast." At the Berry Street Conference Doctor X — remembered how many infants he had baptized that year, and Doctor Y — boasted of the number of tracts they had distributed in the West. At Worcester the Annual Convention argued the terms upon which Persons should be admitted to the Communion and debated the grave question, "Have We a Litany Among Us?"; and in 1853 Doctor Lothrop actually hatched a creed studded with silly phrases about "celestial solicitation" and "the withered veins of humanity." That same year Parker peeped in at the Divinity School and concluded that it was a morgue. "The Egyptian embalmers," he said, "took only seventy days to make a mummy out of a dead man. Unitarian embalmers used three years in making a mummy out of a live one." Doctor Ripley's church looked askance at his ideas of social reform, and Chandler Robbins was proud that no social question had ever intruded itself upon the decorum of his services; the Federal Street Church would not allow Doctor Channing to announce an anti-slavery meeting, and Doctor Frothingham found it hard to understand why anyone should wish to improve a society so nearly perfect. Clergymen stood ready to testify to the good character of a Webster or a Choate, and debated whether Emerson was a Christian; there were separate chapels for the poor, where only the orthodox might preach.

The air of Boston was electric with reform, but the windows of the churches were closed. Yet it was not so elsewhere. Out in Worcester Edward Everett Hale vied with Thomas Wentworth Higginson in the socialization of Christianity; in Syracuse Sam Jo May turned his church over to the radicals; and in New York the talented but eccentric Henry Bellows meddled dangerously with profane affairs. But here in Boston the Unitarians had become respectable and conservative. They were gentlemen and not unaware of the fact; they moved in the best circles, their conduct was dignified and their manners refined. They worshipped reason and loved peace, and enthusiasm they thought vulgar. Norton was their scholar and James Walker their philosopher, and they read Holmes more gladly than Lowell. There had been liberals in the church, but somehow they had disappeared, and now Doctor Lothrop and Doctor Frothingham set the pace. Pierpont had talked too much, and Sargent had been too independent, and both, now, were gone. Parker himself was outside the pale, and when James Freeman Clarke invited him into his pulpit, his wealthiest parishioners seceded to more comfortable pews. Emerson had left the church; Ripley had left the church; Brownson had left the church. And Channing was gone, Channing whose greatness of spirit had encompassed the town.

Who was there to take the place of Channing? Who was there now to preach the Dignity of Man and the religion of Humanity? He was, thought Parker, the greatest clergyman of his time, the greatest man of his time. For forty years his presence had been a benediction to the city, and his piety an inspiration to the Church. His saintliness was a challenge to sin, and his holiness a rebuke to iniquity. He took the highest ground and drew men to him; he made the most audacious assumptions and shamed men into granting them. His idealism was inexorable, his faith in the goodness of man was not to be gainsaid, and when men disappointed him, his grief stung them like conscience. He had not great learning, but he spoke with the authority of law; he had neither brilliance nor wit, but his words flew around the earth.

No one had achieved more for reform than had Channing, who was not afraid to descend from seraphic abstractions to homely applications. He had the innocence of Alcott, but he did not suffer fools gladly nor live in a world of his own imagining; he had the serenity of Emerson, but he was not willing to adjourn the present for the future or to insist upon the proper limits of his own responsibility. His tolerance did not paralyze his moral sensibilities nor his magnanimity cool his passion for righteousness. He made heresy plausible and revolution respectable; he lent dignity to every reform, and clothed the most dangerous doctrines in the garments of gentility.

With every year he grew more radical in his thinking and bolder in his action. The Peace Society of Massachusetts was organized in his study; and in his study, too, Dorothea Dix prepared her moving Memorial on the condition of the insane. He championed penal reform and the abolition of capital punishment, and assured his wealthy parishioners that the criminal caught the infection of vice from the upper classes. He was among the first to celebrate the work of Horace Mann, and he urged the President of Harvard College to provide democratic education for the plain people of the country. He gave his name to a form of Unitarianism, but he had no proprietary interest in the Church and he was more afraid of conformity than of dissent. He supported Father Taylor and encouraged Brownson and welcomed James Freeman Clarke, and at his death the Catholic Church honored the man who had befriended Bishop Cheverus. When Abner Kneeland was jugged for blasphemy, it was Channing who drew up the petition for pardon; when Faneuil Hall was denied to the abolitionists, it was Channing who secured it for them by his Appeal to the Citizens of Boston. He did not fail to countenance by his presence the Chardon Street Convention, and from the platform of Faneuil Hall he denounced the murderers of Elijah Lovejoy. "I have no fear of revolutions," he said, "we have conservative principles enough." He was not a socialist, but no Brook Farmer could have condemned more severely the sins of property; he was not a non-resistant, but no pacifist could have painted more blackly the degradation of war; he was not an abolitionist, but his objections to slavery had carried conviction where Garrison's did not. He was independent of every reform group, but aloof from none; he belonged to no clique but gave strength to them all. He was a leader and a symbol, and now he was gone there was none to take his place. . . .

So Parker came in to join the Boston reformers, to make his peculiar contribution of applied Christianity. His church had been organized just for him, and under no ordinary auspices, and something more was expected than a performance of ritual or an annotation of the Gospels. Not because of his learning or his eloquence, or even his piety, had it been resolved "that the Rev. Theodore Parker shall have a chance to be heard in Boston," but because he was the one spokesman of transcendentalism among the clergy, the one uncompromising critic of Hunkerism in the Church. No one else could do what he was expected to do, not James Freeman Clarke, not Pierpont, nor Sargent, nor young Starr King, for all their good intentions. Among all the Boston clergy Parker was the only one to associate on equal terms with the lay reformers, with Garrison and Mann, Phillips and Howe. And among all the reformers, he was the only one who found it possible to remain in

the Church and to use the pulpit as the vantage ground from which to direct the attack. He had seen the Church become the apologist for the established order, he had seen the leadership in moral progress pass from the clergy to the laity; he remained stubbornly convinced that the Church might yet be made an instrument for social reform, and he was bold enough to assume responsibility for the experiment. He was not a Channing, but he hoped to complete what Channing had inaugurated. Did he anticipate, that winter day of 1846 when he conducted his own installation as Minister of the Twenty-eighth Congregational Society, did he anticipate that preëminence which was to bring him such odium as no other clergyman suffered, such honor as no other clergyman knew, that fame which was to make his name a byword and a benediction? Did he foresee the strange company he was to keep in the coming years, the peculiar causes he was to plead, the power he was to wield? "I did not know what was latent in myself," he wrote years later, "nor foresee all the doctrines which then were hid in my own first principles, what embryo fruit and flowers lay sheathed in the obvious bud." Yet all the future was implicit in that installation sermon on *The True Idea of the Christian Church*.

"A Christian Church," he said, standing there so young and so terribly earnest, so anxious to do justice to his theme and to reach the hearts of the hundreds who had crowded into the great Melodeon, — "A Christian Church should be the means of reforming the world, of forming it after the pattern of Christian ideas. It should therefore bring up the sentiments of the times, the ideas of the times, and the actions of the times, to judge them by the universal standard. We expect the sins of commerce to be winked at in the streets; the sins of the state to be applauded on election day and in a Congress, or on the Fourth of July; we are used to hear them called the righteousness of the nation. You expect them to be tried by passion, which looks only to immediate results and partial ends. Here they are to be measured by Conscience and Reason, which look to permanent results and universal ends; to be looked at with reference to the Laws of God, the everlasting ideas on which alone is based the welfare of the world. If the church be true, many things which seem gainful in the street and expedient in the senate-house, will here be set down as wrong, and all gain which comes therefrom seem to be but a loss. If there be a public sin in the land, if a lie invade the state, it is for the church to give the alarm; it is here that it may war on lies and sin; the more widely they are believed in and practised, the more are they deadly, the more to be opposed. Here let no false idea or false action of the public go without exposure or rebuke. But let no noble heroism of the times, no noble man pass by without due honor."

Nothing was beyond the province of the Church, nothing foreign to its interest or exempt from its control. Its jurisdiction embraced the morals of the State as well as the morals of men, its purpose was the salvation of society as well as the salvation of the individual. Its liturgy was social welfare, its sacraments good works, its creed the perfectibility of man. It was Catholic in its authority, Protestant in its attitude. There was no responsibility it could evade, no duty it could ignore. Every beggar, every pauper, was a reproach, every poorhouse, every jail, a disgrace, and it was hypocrisy to pretend to a religion of love and tolerate the injustices of man to man. For nineteen centuries the Church had preached the doctrine of Brotherly Love; how could it explain the persistence of brutal crime and vengeful punishment, of iniquity committed in the name of Property, and murder sanctioned by the State? Too long had the church been silent in the face of these evils, too long concerned with dogma and sectarian strife, too long the refuge of the powerful and the sanctuary of the strong. What, indeed, had the Church been doing all this time that the almshouses were crowded and the jails full and harlots walked the streets of Boston? What had the Church been doing that slavery was tolerated and war glorified and labor exploited and woman oppressed and the rich suffered to lord it over the poor? What had the Church been doing that the blind were denied light, and the feeble-minded treated like animals, and children allowed to grow up in ignorance and want, toiling long hours in the factories and going to school in crime? "If the church were to waste less time in building its palaces of theological speculation, palaces mainly of straw, and based upon the chaff, it would surely have more time to use in the practical good works of the day."

This was the heroism of the present, the sainthood of the future, not the defense of a creed or the punishment of a heresy, but the philanthropy that toiled for the ignorant and the needy, for the vagrant and the drunkard, the prostitute and the thief. No need for the Church to seek refuge in abstractions, to preach nebulous moral sentiments; here was work enough at hand, here were causes to enlist the energies of every Christian. War against the crime of war, war against the crime of slavery, war against intemperance and vice, against poverty and ignorance and disease. Of what value the triumph of science and of the arts, if morals lag behind? But apply religion to life, sincerely, intelligently, and you could make over society, you could work a real revolution. "We should build up a great state where there was an honorable work for every hand, bread for all mouths, clothing for all backs, culture for every mind, and love and faith in every heart. . . . The noblest monument to Christ, the fairest trophy of religion, is a noble people, where all are well fed and clad, industrious, free, educated, manly, pious, wise and good."

Here was a confession of faith for the church militant, here was a program of practical philanthropy, a pledge for reform. Let no one mistake the purpose for which the Twenty-eighth Congregational Society had been organized, let no one misapprehend the philosophy which inspired its minister. He was done, now, with theological polemics, done with bickering over a Unitarian creed or quarreling over the privilege of an exchange. He had formulated the Articles of Faith; now for a Sacrament of Works. . . .

When it was the Slave Power crowding Kansas with Border Ruffians or striking down Sumner in his Senate seat, Parker was sure that that South was desperate, and he wrote "The Devil is in great wrath because he knoweth that his time is short." Was the North, too, in despair, that it had to resort to Sharpes rifles and to massacre in Potawatomi and that good men applauded the raid on Harper's Ferry? Parker did not really face this question. The aggressions of freedom, he felt, were justified by a different philosophy. These things were no confessions of moral bankruptcy, as with the South. It was not that John Brown's way was the only way. Neither persuasion nor politics had been aban-

doned, this was merely another expedient: if the South could not understand Garrison or Sumner, perhaps it could learn to understand men like John Brown. "We want all sorts of weapons to attack slavery with," Parker wrote to Thayer, when that deluded philanthropist proposed the colonization of the South itself, "the heavy artillery and the light horse which cuts the lines asunder and routs a whole column before they know the enemy is upon them."

He was convinced that only war could settle this matter of slavery, but he did not embrace a foolish consistency and abdicate politics. He was convinced that the Union would not hold together, but he would not go along with Garrison and Phillips in working for its dissolution, not as long as four million Negroes were slaves. War would come, there was no doubt of it; he had been predicting it ever since the Compromise, and because he was so sure of it, he helped to bring it on. He preached the inevitable conflict, he talked of appealing from the parchment of the Constitution to the parchment on the head of a drum, he struck fine gestures and assured his friends that he bought no more books — he needed his money for cannon.

War would come, and within a few years, too, but sufficient unto the day was the evil thereof, and meantime there was some hope in politics. "I think we live in a time when it is a man's *Duty* to attend to political affairs," he had written, and he was never one to neglect his Duty. He was up to his neck in politics, now, and he fancied himself a power behind the scenes; he took himself seriously and he was taken seriously. He went barnstorming around the country and men forgot his heterodoxy and listened to his politics; only Beecher could command a greater audience, only Greeley was more widely read. His acquaintance was immense, it embraced all of the radical politicians of the North, and he did not hesitate to presume upon it. Not since the days of the Puritan theocracy had any clergyman used so lordly a tone. He knew the place of religion and of politics; he knew that it is less worthy to serve Cæsar than to serve God. He could tell all the politicians what to do and ignore the consequences; what had he to do with consequences? When Sumner was elected to the Senate, Parker sat down and wrote him a letter.

You told me once that you were in morals, not in politics. Now I hope you will show that you are still in morals, although in politics. I hope you will be the *senator with a conscience.* I expect you to make mistakes, blunders; but I hope they will be intellectual and not moral; that you will never miss the Right, however you may miss the Expedient . . . I hope you will build on the Rock of Ages, and look to eternity for your justification. You see, my dear Sumner, that I expect much of you, that I expect heroism of the most heroic kind. The moral and manly excellence of all our prominent men is greatly over-rated by the mass of men. You see I try you by a difficult standard and that I am not easily pleased.

And Sumner, the proud Sumner, humorless and didactic, listened courteously to this sermon (he was used to sermons, he wrote them himself), and tried to be the *senator with a conscience.*

When Wilson went to the Senate, Wilson, the Natick cobbler who justified democracy, Parker warned him that he think more of principles and less of political advancement: —

There is only one thing which made me prefer Charles Francis Adams or S. C. Phillips to you. You have been seeking for office with all your might. Now I don't like this hunting for office in foes and still less in my friends. But for this you would have been my first choice for the senatorship . . . Now let me tell you what I think are the dangers of your position, and also what noble things I expect of you.

And Wilson, who was to disappoint so often those expectations, answered meekly: "I sometimes read over the letter you were so kind as to send me. You dealt frankly with me in that letter, and I thank you for it, and I hope to be better and wiser for it. I shall endeavor while in the Senate to act up to my convictions of duty, to do what I feel to be right." But it was not enough, and soon Sumner had to intercede for Wilson: "I fear you are too harsh upon Wilson, and I fear that you and others will help undermine him by furnishing arguments to the lukewarm and the Hunkers. Bear this in mind and be gentle."

But it was not in Parker to be gentle when moral issues were at stake, and Sumner himself was to feel the flick of his whip more than once. "I thought you did not quite do your duty in 1850–51," Parker wrote him, and when he did not speak at Parker's bidding, Mason of Virginia taunted him: "I see my friend Theodore Parker is after you." And so he was, letter after letter, egging him on, and to Howe. "Do you see what imminent deadly peril poor Sumner is in? If he does not speak, he is *dead — dead — dead.*" But Sumner was not dead, and soon he found an opportunity to make the speech that was expected of him, and Parker was quick to write his approval — and careful to qualify it. "You have made a grand speech," he assured the Senator. "It was worth while to go to Congress to make such a speech. You have done what I have all along said you would do, though I lamented that you did not do it long ago." But there was mutual respect behind all of this, and affection too, and when Sumner was assaulted by Brooks, none grieved more deeply than Parker. "I wish that I could have taken the blows on my head," he wrote, but his sympathy for his friend did not becloud his understanding of the significance of the attack. "Slave holders are not fools," he pointed out. "The South never struck down a Northern advocate of a tariff or a defender of the Union. It attacks only the soldiers of freedom, knowing that the controlling power of the North also hates them."

Sumner and Wilson were Parker's Senators, and he had a right to counsel them, but he did not confine himself to the Senators from Massachusetts: he was father-confessor and spiritual adviser to all the leaders of the Free Soil and Republican parties. Did Seward understand the situation, Seward, whom he was grooming for the Presidency? "Dear Sir," Parker wrote him, "It seems to me that the country has got now to such a pass that the people must interfere and take things out of the hands of the politicians who now control them. Allow me to show in extenso what I mean."

And he did, in one long letter after another, and soon Seward was in Boston, canvassing the political situation with Parker, and on his return to Washington he wrote: "I assured Mr. Sumner and Mr. Wilson that I considered Massachusetts at least organized to the cause of Human Nature. In my own thoughts I have constantly supposed that consummation if speedily attained, was to be due to your restless and sagacious and vigorous ability." And when Parker came to New York he told his audience, "There is not at this day a politician so able, so far-sighted, so cautious, so wise, so discriminating as William Henry Seward," — and this even though Mr. Seward had "no drop of Puritan blood in his veins."

With Chase he was on a more familiar footing. "What a noble man Chase is," Parker exclaimed. "He called to see me yesterday. His face is a benediction to any audience; what a fine eye he has." And to Chase himself: "I *do* consider you a great man and a great statesman. If you are not a great statesman, then who is?" Chase could not answer this question, but, not to be outdone, he assured Parker: "I always like to read your heroic utterances." But their relations were not always on this idyllic plane. When Chase failed to rescue the poor fugitive Margaret Garner, Parker tore into him: "I thought the anti-slavery Governor of Ohio would get possession of that noble woman, either by the hocus-pocus of some legal technicality, or else by the *red right arm of Ohio,* and I confess that I was terribly chagrined that it did not turn out so." And he went on to New York and told his audience there, "If three and a half millions of slaves had been white men, do you suppose the affair at Cincinnati would have turned out after that sort? Do you suppose Governor Chase would have said, 'No slavery outside of the slave States, but inside of the slave States, just as much enslavement of Anglo-Saxon men as you please'?" Chase hadn't said any such thing, and he did not hesitate to tell Parker so, and to tell him how wrong he was in this and in other matters. Was Parker disposed to criticize his conduct? He was not satisfied with Parker's conduct, either, and sometimes Parker threw him into despair by his willful intermixing of religious with political radicalism. "Shall I not say to you frankly," Chase wrote, "how much I regret that on the great question of the Divine Origin of the Bible and the Divine Nature of Christ your views are so little in harmony with those of almost all who labour with you in the great cause of Human Enfranchisement and Progress." Yet their friendship weathered these recriminations.

When Chase came to Boston he did not fail to attend the Music Hall, however much he disapproved of the theology which he heard there, and when Parker invaded Ohio he visited the Governor in Columbus and saw his own picture hanging in the dining room and his sermons lying on the table of the Executive Office.

He knew them all and he made his influence felt. He could see things that the politicians could not see, for he was a philosopher; he could say things that the politicians could not say, for he had no career to consider. "The non-political reformer," he pointed out, "is not restricted by any law, any Constitution, any man, nor by the people, because he is not to deal with institutions; he is to make the institutions better. The non-political reformer is to raise the cotton, to spin it into thread, to weave it into web, to prescribe the pattern after which the dress is to be made; and then he is to pass the cloth and the pattern to the political reformer, and say 'Now, Sir, take your shears, and cut it out and make it up.'" Easy enough for Parker, he was good at spinning thread and weaving webs, and better still at prescribing the patterns for the politicians to cut. "Now a word about Kansas . . ." he would write to Senator Hale, and there would follow pages of illegible manuscript for Mr. Hale to decipher. And, "now *my* way of dealing with the nation is this . . ." he would inform Governor Banks (a broken reed, this Banks) and there would be a long disquisition on the character of a political party and the duty of the Republicans to abolish slavery everywhere. Or to William Herndon on the Ottawa debate: "Mr. Lincoln did not meet the issue. He made a technical evasion. That is not the way to fight the battle of Freedom." Parker knew how to fight the battle of Freedom, and he lectured them all on grand strategy and on tactics —

Bancroft and Birney, Palfrey and Mann, Adams and Julian, as well as the great leaders of the party. "Among all my old friends, there is not one that I can consult with the same confidence I can you," Birney assured him; and from Herndon came a letter to Lydia, "He is about the only man living who can hold me steady."

But it was not all a matter of writing letters or of preaching sermons. He tried his hand at practical politics; in '54 he was busy getting up a convention of all the Free States, and the next year he was circulating petitions throughout the North for the removal of those Federal Judges who had ruled wrongly on the Fugitive Slave Bill. When Sumner was attacked, Parker told Hale, "I shall go to the State House as soon as the House meets to see if I can stir up that body to action," and when the Republicans declared that it was not their intention to attack slavery in the States, he wrote, "It is *my* intention as soon as I get the power." His study was a clearinghouse of radical opinion; here men like Chase and Hale could find out for themselves how relevant were the arguments of Garrison and Phillips. Parker knew what was going on in every State, and everywhere he held up the hands of the radicals and cried down compromise. A political realist, he saw the economic bases of politics; an idealist, he refused to recognize them or to accommodate himself to them. He knew that the Whig Party was no less subservient to vested interests than was the Democratic Party to slavery, and he warned his friends of the attempt of the money power to get control of the new Republican Party. He saw even the effect of the new railroads upon the struggle for freedom in the West, but his perspicuity did not lure him into the compromise fatal to Rantoul, nor bring him over to Douglas, and his abiding fear of that statesman was not without effect in heading off the consummation of Greeley's plot to swing the Little Giant over into the Republican Party.

How much influence did Parker exert, after all? Did Sumner need his prodding or Hale his encouragement? Did Seward benefit by his advice, did Chase profit by his warnings? The task of the non-political reformer, he had said, was to create sentiment, to advance ideas, to suggest modes of action. He had stirred up sentiment enough, and he was generous with ideas, but the only mode of action he could suggest, in the end, was agitation, and that led to war, which is what the politicians were trying to avoid. Yet it was something to be in advance of the politicians without breaking the lines of communication as Garrison had broken them. It was something to rebuke timidity and reject compromise and formulate a policy of aggression, to recall men to fundamental principles and denounce a policy of expediency. It was something to be the Conscience of a Party.

Henry David Thoreau: CIVIL DISOBEDIENCE

> *Thoreau's famous essay, originally a lecture twice delivered at the Concord Lyceum, attracted little attention until long after his death. Now, it is influential everywhere and has inspired conscientious objectors of every sort. Gandhi said that it was a source of the formulation of his policies of civil disobedience and non-violent non-cooperation. It was influential among the resistance groups in countries occupied by the Nazis. It is relevant to any argument about the Nuremberg and Eichmann trials, and to the United Nations Universal Declaration of Human Rights. It is invoked by anti-nuclear war picketers and opponents of the war in Vietnam. And it provides the motivating principle for many leaders of the struggle against racial and caste segregation wherever it exists.*
>
> *Thoreau, as is usual with him, states his thesis in the form of a paradox: "Any man more right than his neighbors constitutes a majority of one already." The ambiguity here resides in the word "more." Literally, as Thoreau seems to realize, conscience means a "knowing-with." How, though, does one determine who is the more right? If we are true to ourselves, each of us must affirm that what we believe to be right is so. Thoreau's problem is the everlasting one of him who would admonish another: "And why beholdest thou the mote that is in thy brother's eye, but perceivest not the beam that is in thine own eye?"*

I HEARTILY accept the motto, — "That government is best which governs least"; and I should like to see it acted up to more rapidly and systematically. Carried out, it finally amounts to this, which also I believe, — "That government is best which governs not at all"; and when men are prepared for it, that will be the kind of government which they will have. Government is at best but an expedient; but most governments are usually, and all governments are sometimes, inexpedient. The objections which have been brought against a standing army, and they are many and weighty, and deserve to prevail, may also at last be brought against a standing government. The standing army is only an arm of the standing government. The government itself, which is only the mode which the people have chosen to execute their will, is equally liable to be abused and perverted before the people can act through it. Witness the present Mexican war, the work of comparatively a few individuals using the standing government as their tool; for, in the outset, the people would not have consented to this measure.

This American government, — what is it but a tradition, though a recent one, endeavoring to transmit itself unimpaired to posterity, but each instant losing some of its integrity? It has not the vitality and force of a single living man; for a single man can bend it to his will. It is a sort of wooden gun to the people themselves. But it is not the less necessary for this; for the people must have some complicated machinery or other, and hear its din, to satisfy that idea of government which they have. Governments show thus how successfully men can be imposed on, even impose on themselves, for their own advantage. It is excellent, we must all allow. Yet this government never of itself furthered any enterprise, but by the alacrity with which it got out of its way. *It* does not keep the country free. *It* does not settle the West. *It* does not educate. The character inherent in the American people has done all that has been accomplished; and it would have done somewhat more, if the government had not sometimes got in its way. For government is an expedient by which men would fain succeed in letting one another alone; and, as has been said, when it is most expedient, the governed are most let alone by it. Trade and commerce, if they were not made of India-rubber, would never manage to bounce over the obstacles which legislators are continually putting in their way; and, if one were to judge these men wholly by the effects of their actions and not partly by their intentions, they would deserve to be classed and punished with those mischievous persons who put obstructions on the railroads.

But, to speak practically and as a citizen, unlike those who call themselves no-government men, I ask for, not at once no government, but *at once* a better government. Let every man make known what kind of government would command his respect, and that will be one step toward obtaining it.

After all, the practical reason why, when the power is once in the hands of the people, a majority are permitted, and for a long period continue, to rule is not because they are most likely to be in the right, nor because this seems fairest to the minority, but because they are physically the strongest. But a government in which the majority rule in all cases cannot be based on justice, even as far as men understand it. Can there not be a government in which majorities do not virtually decide right and wrong, but conscience? — in which majorities decide only those questions to which the rule of expediency is applicable? Must the citizen ever for a moment, or in the least degree, resign his conscience to the legislator? Why has every man a conscience, then? I think that we should be men first, and subjects afterward. It is not desirable to cultivate a respect for the law, so much as for the right. The only obligation which I have a right to assume is to do at any time what I think right. It is truly enough said, that a corporation has no conscience; but a corporation of conscientious men is a corporation *with* a conscience. Law never made men a whit more just; and, by means of their respect for it, even the well-disposed are daily made the agents of injustice. A common and natural result of an undue respect for law is, that you may see a file of soldiers, colonel, captain, corporal, privates, powder-monkeys, and all, marching in admirable order over hill and dale to the wars, against their wills, ay, against their common sense and consciences, which makes it very steep marching indeed, and produces a palpitation of the heart. They have no doubt that it is a damnable business in which they are concerned; they are all peaceably inclined. Now, what are they? Men at all? or small movable forts and magazines, at the service of some unscrupulous man in power? Visit the Navy-Yard, and behold a marine, such a man as an American government can make, or such as it can make a man with its black arts, — a mere shadow and reminiscence of humanity, a man laid out alive and standing, and already, as one may say, buried under arms with funeral accompaniments, though it may be, —

Not a drum was heard, not a funeral note,
    As his corse to the rampart we hurried;
Not a soldier discharged his farewell shot
    O'er the grave where our hero we buried.

The mass of men serve the state thus, not as men mainly, but as machines, with their bodies. They are the standing army, and the militia, jailers, constables, posse comitatus, etc. In most cases there is no free exercise whatever of the judgment or of the moral sense; but they put themselves on a level with wood and earth and stones; and wooden men can perhaps be manufactured that will serve the purpose as well. Such command no more respect than men of straw or a lump of dirt. They have the same sort of worth only as horses and dogs. Yet such as these even are commonly esteemed good citizens. Others — as most legislators, politicians, lawyers, ministers, and officeholders — serve the state chiefly with their heads; and, as they rarely make any moral distinctions, they are as likely to serve the Devil, without *intending* it, as God. A very few, as heroes, patriots, martyrs, reformers in the great sense, and *men*, serve the state with their consciences also, and so necessarily resist it for the most part; and they are commonly treated as enemies by it. A wise man will only be useful as a man, and will not submit to be "clay," and "stop a hole to keep the wind away," but leave that office to his dust at least:

I am too high-born to be propertied,
To be a secondary at control,
Or useful serving-man and instrument
To any sovereign state throughout the world.

He who gives himself entirely to his fellow-men appears to them useless and selfish; but he who gives himself partially to them is pronounced a benefactor and philanthropist.

How does it become a man to behave toward this American government today? I answer, that he cannot without disgrace be associated with it. I cannot for an instant recognize that political organization as *my* government which is the *slave's* government also.

All men recognize the right of revolution; that is, the right to refuse allegiance to, and to resist, the government, when its tyranny or its inefficiency are great and unendurable. But almost all say that such is not the case now. But such was the case, they think, in the Revolution of '75. If one were to tell me that this was a bad government because it taxed certain foreign commodities brought to its ports, it is most probable that I should not make an ado about it, for I can do without them. All machines have their friction; and possibly this does enough good to counterbalance the evil. At any rate, it is a great evil to make a stir about it. But when the friction comes to have its machine, and oppression and robbery are organized, I say, let us not have such a machine any longer. In other words, when a sixth of the population of a nation which has undertaken to be the refuge of liberty are slaves, and a whole country is unjustly overrun and conquered by a foreign army, and subjected to military law, I think that it is not too soon for honest men to rebel and revolutionize. What makes this duty the more urgent is the fact that the country so overrun is not our own, but ours is the invading army.

Paley, a common authority with many on moral questions, in his chapter on the "Duty of Submission to Civil Government," resolves all civil obligation into expediency; and he proceeds to say, "that so long as the interest of the whole society requires it, that is, so long as the established government cannot be resisted or changed without public inconveniency, it is the will of God that the established government be obeyed, and no longer. . . . This principle being admitted, the justice of every particular case of resistance is reduced to a computation of the quantity of the danger and grievance on the one side, and of the probability and expense of redressing it on the other." Of this, he says, every man shall judge for himself. But Paley appears never to have contemplated those

cases to which the rule of expediency does not apply, in which a people, as well as an individual, must do justice, cost what it may. If I have unjustly wrested a plank from a drowning man, I must restore it to him though I drown myself. This, according to Paley, would be inconvenient. But he that would save his life, in such a case, shall lose it. This people must cease to hold salves, and to make war on Mexico, though it cost them their existence as a people.

In their practice, nations agree with Paley; but does any one think that Massachusetts does exactly what is right at the present crisis?

A drab of state, a cloth-o'-silver slut,
To have her train borne up, and her soul trail
    in the dirt.

Practically speaking, the opponents to a reform in Massachusetts are not a hundred thousand politicians at the South, but a hundred thousand merchants and farmers here, who are more interested in commerce and agriculture than they are in humanity, and are not prepared to do justice to the slave and to Mexico, *cost what it may*. I quarrel not with far-off foes, but with those who, near at home, cooperate with, and do the bidding of, those far away, and without whom the latter would be harmless. We are accustomed to say, that the mass of men are unprepared; but improvement is slow, because the few are not materially wiser or better than the many. It is not so important that many should be as good as you, as that there be some absolute goodness somewhere; for that will leaven the whole lump. There are thousands who are *in opinion* opposed to slavery and to the war, who yet in effect do nothing to put an end to them; who, esteeming themselves children of Washington and Franklin, sit down with their hands in their pockets, and say that they know not what to do, and do nothing; who even postpone the question of freedom to the question of free-trade, and quietly read the prices-current along with the latest advices from Mexico, after dinner, and, it may be, fall asleep over them both. What is the price-current of an honest man and patriot to-day? They hesitate, and they regret, and sometimes they petition; but they do nothing in earnest and with effect. They will wait, well disposed, for others to remedy the evil, that they may no longer have it to regret. At most, they give only a cheap vote, and a feeble countenance and Godspeed, to the right, as it goes by them. There are nine hundred and ninety-nine patrons of virtue to one virtuous man. But it is easier to deal with the real possessor of a thing than with the temporary guardian of it.

All voting is a sort of gaming, like checkers or backgammon, with a slight moral tinge to it, a playing with right and wrong, with moral questions; and betting naturally accompanies it. The character of the voters is not staked. I cast my vote, perchance, as I think right; but I am not vitally concerned that that right should prevail. I am willing to leave it to the majority. Its obligation, therefore, never exceeds that of expediency. Even voting *for the right* is *doing* nothing for it. It is only expressing to men feebly your desire that it should prevail. A wise man will not leave the right to the mercy of chance, nor wish it to prevail through the power of majority. There is but little virtue in the action of masses of men. When the majority shall at length vote for the abolition of slavery, it will be because they are indifferent to slavery, or because there is but little slavery left to be abolished by their vote. *They* will then be the only slaves. Only *his* vote can hasten the abolition of slav-

ery who asserts his own freedom by his vote.

I hear of a convention to be held at Baltimore, or elsewhere, for the selection of a candidate for the Presidency, made up chiefly of editors, and men who are politicians by profession; but I think, what is it to any independent, intelligent, and respectable man what decision they may come to? Shall we not have the advantage of his wisdom and honesty, nevertheless? Can we not count upon some independent votes? Are there not many individuals in the country who do not attend conventions? But no: I find that the respectable man, so called, has immediately drifted from his position, and despairs of his country, when his country has more reason to despair of him. He forthwith adopts one of the candidates thus selected as the only *available* one, thus proving that he is himself *available* for any purposes of the demagogue. His vote is of no more worth than that of any unprincipled foreigner or hireling native, who may have been bought. O for a man who is a *man,* and, as my neighbor says, has a bone in his back which you cannot pass your hand through! Our statistics are at fault: the population has been returned too large. How many *men* are there to a square thousand miles in this country? Hardly one. Does not America offer any inducement for men to settle here? The American has dwindled into an Odd Fellow, — one who may be known by the development of his organ of gregariousness, and a manifest lack of intellect and cheerful self-reliance; whose first and chief concern, on coming into the world, is to see that the Alms-houses are in good repair; and, before yet he has lawfully donned the virile garb, to collect a fund for the support of the widows and orphans that may be; who, in short, ventures to live only by the aid of the Mutual Insurance company, which has promised to bury him decently.

It is not a man's duty, as a matter of course, to devote himself to the eradication of any, even the most enormous wrong; he may still properly have other concerns to engage him; but it is his duty, at least, to wash his hands of it, and, if he gives it no thought longer, not to give it practically his support. If I devote myself to other pursuits and contemplations, I must first see, at least, that I do not pursue them sitting upon another man's shoulders. I must get off him first, that he may pursue his contemplations too. See what gross inconsistency is tolerated. I have heard some of my townsmen say, "I should like to have them order me out to help put down an insurrection of the slaves, or to march to Mexico; — see if I would go"; and yet these very men have each, directly by their allegiance, and so indirectly, at least, by their money, furnished a substitute. The soldier is applauded who refuses to serve in an unjust war by those who do not refuse to sustain the unjust government which makes the war; is applauded by those whose own act and authority he disregards and sets at naught; as if the state were penitent to that degree that it hired one to scourge it while it sinned, but not to that degree that it left off sinning for a moment. Thus, under the name of Order and Civil Government, we are all made at last to pay homage to and support our own meanness. After the first blush of sin comes its indifference; and from immoral it becomes, as it were, *un*moral, and not quite unnecessary to that life which we have made.

The broadest and most prevalent error requires the most disinterested virtue to sustain it. The slight reproach to which the virtue of patriotism is commonly liable, the noble are most likely to incur. Those who, while they disapprove of the character and measures of a government, yield to it their allegiance and support are undoubtedly its most conscientious supporters, and so frequently the most serious obstacles to reform. Some are petitioning the state to dissolve the Union, to disregard the requisitions of the President. Why do they not dissolve it themselves, — the union between themselves and the state, — and refuse to pay their quota into its treasury? Do not they stand in the same relation to the state that the state does to the Union? And have not the same reasons prevented the state from resisting the Union which have prevented them from resisting the state?

How can a man be satisfied to entertain an opinion merely, and enjoy *it*? Is there any enjoyment in it, if his opinion is that he is aggrieved? If you are cheated out of a single dollar by your neighbor, you do not rest satisfied with knowing that you are cheated, or with saying that you are cheated, or even with petitioning him to pay you your due; but you take effectual steps at once to obtain the full amount, and see that you are never cheated again. Action from principle, the perception and the performance of right, changes things and relations; it is essentially revolutionary, and does not consist wholly with anything which was. It not only divides states and churches, it divides families; ay, it divides the *individual*, separating the diabolical in him from the divine.

Unjust laws exist: shall we be content to obey them, or shall we endeavor to amend them, and obey them until we have succeeded, or shall we transgress them at once? Men generally, under such a government as this, think that they ought to wait until they have persuaded the majority to alter them. They think that, if they should resist, the remedy would be worse than the evil. But it is the fault of the government itself that the remedy *is* worse than the evil. *It* makes it worse. Why is it not more apt to anticipate and provide for reform? Why does it not cherish its wise minority? Why does it cry and resist before it is hurt? Why does it not encourage its citizens to be on the alert to point out its faults, and *do* better than it would have them? Why does it always crucify Christ, and excommunicate Copernicus and Luther, and pronounce Washington and Franklin rebels?

One would think, that a deliberate and practical denial of its authority was the only offense never contemplated by government; else, why has it not assigned its definite, its suitable and proportionate penalty? If a man who has no property refuses but once to earn nine shillings for the state, he is put in prison for a period unlimited by any law that I know, and determined only by the discretion of those who placed him there; but if he should steal ninety times nine shillings from the state, he is soon permitted to go at large again.

If the injustice is part of the necessary friction of the machine of government, let it go, let it go: perchance it will wear smooth,—certainly the machine will wear out. If the injustice has a spring, or a pulley, or a rope, or a crank, exclusively for itself, then perhaps you may consider whether the remedy will not be worse than the evil; but if it is of such a nature that it requires you to be the agent of injustice to another, then, I say, break the law. Let your life be a counter friction to stop the machine. What I have to do is to see, at any rate, that I do not lend myself to the wrong which I condemn.

As for adopting the ways which the state has provided for remedying the evil, I know not of such ways. They take too much time, and a man's life will be gone. I have other affairs to attend to. I came into this world, not chiefly to make this a good place to live in, but to live in it, be it good or bad. A man has not everything to do, but something; and because he cannot do *everything*, it is not necessary that he should do *something* wrong. It is not my business to be petitioning the Governor or the Legislature any more than it is theirs to petition me; and if they should not hear my petition, what should I do then? But in this case the state has provided no way: its very Constitution is the evil. This may seem to be harsh and stubborn and unconciliatory; but it is to treat with the utmost kindness and consideration the only spirit that can appreciate or deserves it. So is all change for the better, like birth and death, which convulse the body.

I do not hesitate to say, that those who call themselves Abolitionists should at once effectually withdraw their support, both in person and property, from the government of Massachusetts, and not wait till they constitute a majority of one, before they suffer the right to prevail through them. I think that it is enough if they have God on their side, without waiting for that other one. Moreover, any man more right than his neighbors constitutes a majority of one already.

I meet this American government, or its representative, the state government, directly, and face to face, once a year — no more — in the person of its tax-gatherer; this is the only mode in which a man situated as I am necessarily meets it; and it then says distinctly, Recognize me; and the simplest, the most effectual, and, in the present posture of affairs, the indispensablest mode of treating with it on this head, of expressing your little satisfaction with and love for it, is to deny it then. My civil neighbor, the tax-gatherer, is the very man I have to deal with, — for it is, after all, with men and not with parchment that I quarrel, — and he has voluntarily chosen to be an agent of the government. How shall he ever know well what he is and does as an officer of the government, or as a man, until he is obliged to consider whether he shall treat me, his neighbor, for whom he has respect, as a neighbor and well-disposed man, or as a maniac and disturber of the peace, and see if he can get over this obstruction to his neighborliness without a ruder and more impetuous thought or speech corresponding with his action. I know this well, that if one thousand, if one hundred, if ten men whom I could name, — if ten *honest* men only, — ay, if *one* HONEST man, in this State of Massachusetts, *ceasing to hold slaves*, were actually to withdraw from this copartnership, and be locked up in the county jail therefor, it would be the abolition of slavery in America. For it matters not how small the beginning may seem to be: what is once well done is done forever. But we love better to talk about it: that we say is our mission. Reform keeps many scores of newspapers in its service, but not one man. If my esteemed neighbor, the State's ambassador, who will devote his days to the settlement of the question of human rights in the Council Chamber, instead of being threatened with the prisons of Carolina, were to sit down the prisoner of Massachusetts, that State which is so anxious to foist the sin of slavery upon her sister, — though at present she can discover only an act of inhospitality to be the ground of a quarrel with her, — the Legislature would not wholly waive the subject the following winter.

Under a government which imprisons any unjustly, the true place for a just man is also a prison. The proper place to-day, the only place which Massachusetts has provided for her free and less desponding spirit, is in her prisons, to be put out and locked out of the State by her own act, as they have already put themselves out by their principles. It is there that the fugitive slave, and the Mexican prisoner on parole, and the Indian come to plead the wrongs of his race should find them; on that separate, but more free and honorable ground, where the State places those who are not *with* her, but *against* her, — the only house in a slave State in which a free man can abide with honor. If any think that their influence would be lost there, and their voices no longer afflict the ear of the State, that they would not be as an enemy within its walls, they do not know by how much truth is stronger than error, nor how much more eloquently and effectively he can combat injustice who has experienced a little in his own person. Cast your whole vote, not a strip of paper merely, but your whole influence. A minority is powerless while it conforms to the majority; it is not even a minority then; but it is irresistible when it clogs by its whole weight. If the alternative is to keep all just men in prison, or give up war and slavery, the State will not hesitate which to choose. If a thousand men were not to pay their tax-bills this year, that would not be a violent and bloody measure, as it would be to pay them, and enable the State to commit violence and shed innocent blood. This is, in fact, the definition of a peaceable revolution, if any such is possible. If the tax-gatherer, or any other public officer, asks me, as one has done, "But what shall I do?" my answer is, "If you really wish to do anything, resign your office." When the subject has refused allegiance, and the officer has resigned his office, then the revolution is accomplished. But even suppose blood should flow. Is there not a sort of blood shed when the conscience is wounded? Through this wound a man's real manhood and immortality flow out, and he bleeds to an everlasting death. I see this blood flowing now.

I have contemplated the imprisonment of the offender, rather than the seizure of his goods, — though both will serve the same purpose, — because they who assert the purest right, and consequently are most dangerous to a corrupt State, commonly have not spent much time in accumulating property. To such the State renders comparatively small service, and a slight tax is wont to appear exorbitant, particularly if they are obliged to earn it by special labor with their hands. If there were one who lived wholly without the use of money, the State itself would hesitate to demand it of him. But the rich man — not to make any invidious comparison — is always sold to the institution which makes him rich. Absolutely speaking, the more money, the less virtue; for money comes between a man and his objects, and obtains them for him; and it was certainly no great virtue to obtain it. It puts to rest many questions which he would otherwise be taxed to answer; while the only new question which it puts is the hard but superfluous one, how to spend it. Thus his moral ground is taken from under his feet. The opportunities of living are diminished in proportion as what are called the "means" are increased. The best thing a man can do for his culture when he is rich is to endeavor to carry out those schemes which he entertained when he was poor. Christ answered the Herodians according to their condition. "Show me the tribute-money," said he; — and one took

a penny out of his pocket; — if you use money which has the image of Caesar on it, and which he has made current and valuable, that is, *if you are men of the State*, and gladly enjoy the advantages of Caesar's government, then pay him back some of his own when he demands it. "Render therefore to Caesar that which is Caesar's, and to God those things which are God's," — leaving them no wiser than before as to which was which; for they did not wish to know.

When I converse with the freest of my neighbors, I perceive that, whatever they may say about the magnitude and seriousness of the question, and their regard for the public tranquillity, the long and short of the matter is, that they cannot spare the protection of the existing government, and they dread the consequences to their property and families of disobedience to it. For my own part, I should not like to think that I ever rely on the protection of the State. But, if I deny the authority of the State when it presents its tax-bill, it will soon take and waste all my property, and so harass me and my children without end. This is hard. This makes it impossible for a man to live honestly, and at the same time comfortably, in outward respects. It will not be worth the while to accumulate property; that would be sure to go again. You must hire or squat somewhere, and raise but a small crop, and eat that soon. You must live within yourself, and depend upon yourself always tucked up and ready for a start, and not have many affairs. A man may grow rich in Turkey even, if he will be in all respects a good subject of the Turkish government. Confucius said: "If a state is governed by the principles of reason, poverty and misery are subjects of shame; if a state is not governed by the principles of reason, riches and honors are the subjects of shame." No: until I want the protection of Massachusetts to be extended to me in some distant Southern port, where my liberty is endangered, or until I am bent solely on building up an estate at home by peaceful enterprise, I can afford to refuse allegiance to Massachusetts, and her right to my property and life. It costs me less in every sense to incur the penalty of disobedience to the State than it would to obey. I should feel as if I were worth less in that case.

Some years ago, the State met me in behalf of the Church, and commanded me to pay a certain sum toward the support of a clergyman whose preaching my father attended, but never I myself. "Pay," it said, "or be locked up in the jail." I declined to pay. But, unfortunately, another man saw fit to pay it. I did not see why the schoolmaster should be taxed to support the priest, and not the priest the schoolmaster; for I was not the State's schoolmaster, but I supported myself by voluntary subscription. I did not see why the lyceum should not present its tax-bill, and have the State to back its demand, as well as the Church. However, at the request of the selectmen, I condescended to make some such statement as this in writing: — "Know all men by these presents, that I, Henry Thoreau, do not wish to be regarded as a member of any incorporated society which I have not joined." This I gave to the town clerk; and he has it. The State, having thus learned that I did not wish to be regarded as a member of that church, has never made a like demand on me since; though it said that it must adhere to its original presumption that time. If I had known how to name them, I should then have signed off in detail from all the societies which I never signed onto; but I did not know where to find a complete list.

I have paid no poll-tax for six years. I was put into a jail once on this account, for one night; and, as I stood considering the walls of solid stone, two or three feet thick, the door of wood and iron, a foot thick, and the iron grating which strained the light, I could not help being struck with the foolishness of that institution which treated me as if I were mere flesh and blood and bones, to be locked up. I wondered that it should have concluded at length that this was the best use it could put me to, and had never thought to avail itself of my services in some way. I saw that, if there was a wall of stone between me and my townsmen, there was a still more difficult one to climb or break through before they could get to be as free as I was. I did not for a moment feel confined, and the walls seemed a great waste of stone and mortar. I felt as if I alone of all my townsmen had paid my tax. They plainly did not know how to treat me, but behaved like persons who are underbred. In every threat and in every compliment there was a blunder; for they thought that my chief desire was to stand the other side of that stone wall. I could not but smile to see how industriously they locked the door on my meditations, which followed them out again without let or hindrance, and *they* were really all that was dangerous. As they could not reach me, they had resolved to punish my body; just as boys, if they cannot come at some person against whom they have a spite, will abuse his dog. I saw that the State was half-witted, that it was timid as a lone woman with her silver spoons, and that it did not know its friends from its foes, and I lost all my remaining respect for it, and pitied it.

Thus the State never intentionally confronts a man's sense, intellectual or moral, but only his body, his senses. It is not armed with superior wit or honesty, but with superior physical strength. I was not born to be forced. I will breathe after my own fashion. Let us see who is the strongest. What force has a multitude? They only can force me who obey a higher law than I. They force me to become like themselves. I do not hear of *men* being *forced* to live this way or that by masses of men. What sort of life were that to live? When I meet a government which says to me, "Your money or your life," why should I be in haste to give it my money? It may be in a great strait, and not know what to do: I cannot help that. It must help itself; do as I do. It is not worth the while to snivel about it. I am not responsible for the successful working of the machinery of society. I am not the son of the engineer. I perceive that, when an acorn and a chestnut fall side by side, the one does not remain inert to make way for the other, but both obey their own laws, and spring and grow and flourish as best they can, till one, perchance, overshadows and destroys the other. If a plant cannot live according to its nature, it dies; and so a man.

The night in prison was novel and interesting enough. The prisoners in their shirt-sleeves were enjoying a chat and the evening air in the doorway, when I entered. But the jailer said, "Come, boys, it is time to lock up"; and so they dispersed, and I heard the sound of their steps returning into the hollow apartments. My roommate was introduced to me by the jailer as "a first-rate fellow and a clever man." When the door was locked, he showed me where to hang my hat, and how he managed matters there. The rooms were whitewashed once a month; and this one, at least, was the whitest, most simply furnished, and probably the neatest apartment in the town.

He naturally wanted to know where I came from, and what brought me there; and, when I had told him, I asked him in my turn how he came there, presuming him to be an honest man, of course; and, as the world goes, I believe he was. "Why," said he, "they accuse me of burning a barn; but I never did it." As near as I could discover, he had probably gone to bed in a barn when drunk, and smoked his pipe there; and so a barn was burnt. He had the reputation of being a clever man, had been there some three months waiting for his trial to come on, and would have to wait as much longer; but he was quite domesticated and contented, since he got his board for nothing, and thought that he was well treated.

He occupied one window, and I the other; and I saw that if one stayed there long, his principal business would be to look out the window. I had soon read all the tracts that were left there, and examined where former prisoners had broken out, and where a grate had been sawed off, and heard the history of the various occupants of that room; for I found that even here there was a history and a gossip which never circulated beyond the walls of the jail. Probably this is the only house in the town where verses are composed, which are afterward printed in a circular form, but not published. I was shown quite a long list of verses which were composed by some young men who had been detected in an attempt to escape, who avenged themselves by singing them.

I pumped my fellow-prisoner as dry as I could, for fear I should never see him again; but at length he showed me which was my bed, and left me to blow out the lamp.

It was like traveling into a far country, such as I had never expected to behold, to lie there for one night. It seemed to me that I never had heard the town-clock strike before, nor the evening sounds of the village; for we slept with the windows open, which were inside the grating. It was to see my native village in the light of the Middle Ages, and our Concord was turned into a Rhine stream, and visions of knights and castles passed before me. They were the voices of old burghers that I heard in the streets. I was an involuntary spectator and auditor of whatever was done and said in the kitchen of the adjacent village-inn, — a wholly new and rare experience to me. It was a closer view of my native town. I was fairly inside of it. I never had seen its institutions before. This is one of its peculiar institutions; for it is a shire town. I began to comprehend what its inhabitants were about.

In the morning, our breakfasts were put through the hole in the door, in small oblong-square tin pans, made to fit, and holding a pint of chocolate, with brown bread, and an iron spoon. When they called for the vessels again, I was green enough to return what bread I had left; but my comrade seized it, and said that I should lay that up for lunch or dinner. Soon after he was let out to work at haying in a neighboring field, whither he went every day, and would not be back till noon; so he bade me goodday, saying that he doubted if he should see me again.

When I came out of prison, — for some one interfered, and paid that tax, — I did not perceive that great changes had taken place on the common, such as he observed who went in a youth and emerged a tottering and gray-headed man; and yet a change had to my eyes come over the scene, — the town, and State, and country, — greater than any that mere time could effect. I saw yet more distinctly the State in which I lived. I saw to what extent the people among whom I lived could be trusted as good neighbors and friends, that their friendship was for summer weather only; that they did not greatly propose to do right; that they were a distinct race from me by their prejudices and superstitions, as the Chinamen and Malays are; that in their sacrifices to humanity they ran no risks, not even to their property; that after all they were not so noble but they treated the thief as he had treated them, and hope, by a certain outward observance and a few prayers, and by walking in a particular straight though useless path from time to time, to save their souls. This may be to judge my neighbors harshly; for I believe that many of them are not aware that they have such an institution as the jail in their village.

It was formerly the custom in our village when a poor debtor came out of jail, for his acquaintances to salute him, looking through their fingers, which were crossed to represent the grating of a jail window, "How do ye do?" My neighbors did not thus salute me, but first looked at me, and then at one another, as if I had returned from a long journey. I was put into jail as I was going to the shoemaker's to get a shoe which was mended. When I was let out the next morning, I proceeded to finish my errand, and, having put on my mended shoe, joined a huckleberry party, who were impatient to put themselves under my conduct; and in half an hour, — for the horse was soon tackled, — was in the midst of a huckleberry field, on one of our highest hills, two miles off, and then the State was nowhere to be seen.

This is the whole history of "My Prisons."

I have never declined paying the highway tax, because I am as desirous of being a good neighbor as I am of being a bad subject; and as for supporting schools, I am doing my part to educate my fellow-countrymen now. It is for no particular item in the tax-bill that I refuse to pay it. I simply wish to refuse allegiance to the State, to withdraw and stand aloof from it effectually. I do not care to trace the course of my dollar, if I could, till it buys a man or a musket to shoot one with, — the dollar is innocent, — but I am concerned to trace the effects of my allegiance. In fact, I quietly declare war with the State, after my fashion, though I will still make what use and get what advantage of her I can, as is usual in such cases.

If others pay the tax which is demanded of me, from a sympathy with the State, they do but what they have already done in their own case, or rather they abet injustice to a greater extent than the State requires. If they pay the tax from a mistaken interest in the individual taxed, to save his property, or prevent his going to jail, it is because they have not considered wisely how far they let their private feelings interfere with the public good.

This, then, is my position at present. But one cannot be too much on his guard in such a case, lest his action be biased by obstinacy or an undue regard for the opinions of men. Let him see that he does only what belongs to himself and to the hour.

I think sometimes, Why, this people mean well, they are only ignorant; they would do better if they knew how: why give your neighbors this pain to treat you as they are not inclined to? But I think again, this is no reason why I should do as they do, or permit others to suffer much greater pain of a different kind. Again, I sometimes say to myself,

When many millions of men, without heat, without ill will, without personal feeling of any kind, demand of you a few shillings only, without the possibility, such is their constitution, of retracting or altering their present demand, and without the possibility, on your side, of appeal to any other millions, why expose yourself to this overwhelming brute force? You do not resist cold and hunger, the winds and the waves, thus obstinately; you quietly submit to a thousand similar necessities. You do not put your head into the fire. But just in proportion as I regard this as not wholly a brute force, but partly a human force, and consider that I have relations to those millions as to so many millions of men, and not of mere brute or inanimate things, I see that appeal is possible, first and instantaneously, from them to the Maker of them, and, secondly, from them to themselves. But if I put my head deliberately into the fire, there is no appeal to fire or to the Maker of fire, and I have only myself to blame. If I could convince myself that I have any right to be satisfied with men as they are, and to treat them accordingly, and not according, in some respects, to my requisitions and expectations of what they and I ought to be, then, like a good Mussulman and fatalists, I should endeavor to be satisfied with things as they are, and say it is the will of God. And, above all, there is this difference between resisting this and a purely brute or natural force, that I can resist this with some effect; but I cannot expect, like Orpheus, to change the nature of the rocks and trees and beasts.

I do not wish to quarrel with any man or nation. I do not wish to split hairs, to make fine distinctions, or set myself up as better than my neighbors. I seek rather, I may say, even an excuse for conforming to the laws of the land. I am but too ready to conform to them. Indeed, I have reason to suspect myself on this head; and each year, as the tax-gatherer comes round, I find myself disposed to review the acts and position of the general and State governments, and the spirit of the people, to discover a pretext for conformity.

We must affect our country as our parents,
And if at any time we alienate
Our love or industry from doing it honor,
We must respect effects and teach the soul
Matter of conscience and religion,
And not desire of rule or benefit.

I believe that the State will soon be able to take all my work of this sort out of my hands, and then I shall be no better a patriot than my fellow-countrymen. Seen from a lower point of view, the Constitution, with all its faults, is very good; the law and the courts are very respectable; even this State and this American government are, in many respects, very admirable, and rare things, to be thankful for, such as a great many have described them; but seen from a point of view a little higher, they are what I have described them; seen from higher still, and the highest, who shall say what they are, or that they are worth looking at or thinking of at all?

However, the government does not concern me much, and I shall bestow the fewest possible thoughts on it. It is not many moments that I live under a government, even in this world. If a man is thought-free, fancy-free, imagination-free, that which *is not* never for a long time appearing *to be* to him, unwise rulers or reformers cannot fatally interrupt him.

I know that most men think differently from myself; but those whose lives are by profession devoted to the study of these or kindred subjects content me as little as any. Statesmen and legislators, standing so completely within the institution, never distinctly and nakedly behold it. They speak of moving society, but have no resting-place without it. They may be men of a certain experience and discrimination, and have no doubt invented ingenious and even useful systems, for which we sincerely thank them; but all their wit and usefulness lie within certain not very wide limits. They are wont to forget that the world is not governed by policy and expediency. Webster never goes behind government, and so cannot speak with authority about it. His words are wisdom to those legislators who contemplate no essential reform in the existing government; but for thinkers, and those who legislate for all time, he never once glances at the subject. I know of those whose serene and wise speculations on this theme would soon reveal the limits of his mind's range and hospitality. Yet, compared with the cheap professions of most reformers, and the still cheaper wisdom and eloquence of politicians in general, his are almost the only sensible and valuable words, and we thank Heaven for him. Comparatively, he is always strong, original, and, above all, practical. Still, his quality is not wisdom, but prudence. The lawyer's truth is not Truth, but consistency or a consistent expediency. Truth is always in harmony with herself, and is not concerned chiefly to reveal the justice that may consist with wrong-doing. He well deserves to be called, as he has been called, the Defender of the Constitution. There are really no blows to be given by him but defensive ones. He is not a leader, but a follower. His leaders are the men of '87. "I have never made an effort," he says, "and never propose to make an effort; I have never countenanced an effort, and never mean to countenance an effort, to disturb the arrangement as originally made, by which the various States came into the Union." Still thinking of the sanction which the Constitution gives to slavery, he says, "Because it was a part of the original compact, — let it stand." Notwithstanding his special acuteness and ability, he is unable to take a fact out of its merely political relations, and behold it as it lies absolutely to be disposed of by the intellect, — what, for instance, it behooves a man to do here in America to-day with regard to slavery, — but ventures, or is driven, to make some such desperate answer as the following, while professing to speak absolutely, and as a private man, — from which what new and singular code of social duties might be inferred? "The manner," says he, "in which the governments of those States where slavery exists are to regulate it is for their own consideration, under their responsibility to their constituents, to the general laws of propriety, humanity, and justice, and to God. Associations formed elsewhere, springing from a feeling of humanity, or any other cause, have nothing whatever to do with it. They have never received any encouragement from me, and they never will."

They who know of no purer sources of truth, who have traced up its stream no higher, stand, and wisely stand, by the Bible and the Constitution, and drink at it there with reverence and humility; but they who behold where it comes trickling into this lake or that pool, gird up their loins once more, and continue their pilgrimage toward its fountainhead.

No man with a genius for legislation has appeared in America. They are rare in the history of the world. There are orators, politicians, and eloquent men, by the thousand; but the speaker has not yet opened his mouth to speak who is capable of settling the much-vexed questions of the day. We love eloquence for its own sake, and not for any truth which it may utter, or any heroism it may inspire. Our legislators have not yet learned the comparative value of free-trade and of freedom, of union, and of rectitude, to a nation. They have no genius or talent for comparatively humble questions of taxation and finance, commerce and manufactures and agriculture. If we were left solely to the wordy wit of legislators in Congress for our guidance, uncorrected by the seasonable experience and the effectual complaints of the people, America would not long retain her rank among the nations. For eighteen hundred years, though perchance I have no right to say it, the New Testament has been written; yet where is the legislator who has wisdom and practical talent enough to avail himself of the light which it sheds on the science of legislation?

The authority of government, even such as I am willing to submit to, — for I will cheerfully obey those who know and can do better than I, and in many things even those who neither know nor can do so well, — is still an impure one: to be strictly just, it must have the sanction and consent of the governed. It can have no pure right over my person and property but what I concede to it. The progress from an absolute to a limited monarchy, from a limited monarchy to a democracy, is a progress toward a true respect for the individual. Even the Chinese philosopher was wise enough to regard the individual as the basis of the empire. Is a democracy, such as we know it, the last improvement possible in government? Is it not possible to take a step further towards recognizing and organizing the rights of man? There will never be a really free and enlightened State until the State comes to recognize the individual as a higher and independent power, from which all its own power and authority are derived, and treats him accordingly. I please myself with imagining a State at last which can afford to be just to all men, and to treat the individual with respect as a neighbor; which even would not think it inconsistent with its own repose if a few were to live aloof from it, not meddling with it, nor embraced by it, who fulfilled all the duties of neighbors and fellow-men. A State which bore this kind of fruit, and suffered it to drop off as fast as it ripened, would prepare the way for a still more perfect and glorious State, which also I have imagined, but not yet anywhere seen.

Max Lerner: THOREAU: NO HERMIT

Max Lerner is one of the most versatile political scientists of our generation. In addition to teaching at several colleges and universities, he was a columnist for the short-lived New York Star, *and served as an editor of the* Nation. *He is now Professor of American Civilization at Brandeis University.*

In this brief essay Professor Lerner warns us that Thoreau's "hermit-like individualism may easily be overemphasized, just as his absorption with nature has been overemphasized. Both must be seen as part of a rebellion against the oversocialized New England town, in which the individual was being submerged, and against the factory system which saw nature only as so much raw material and sought to subdue it to the uses of profit." Conscientious protest is, for Thoreau, he thinks, a mode of educating his fellow citizens, of making them more conscientious. In this he was only following — though in a more rigid and uncompromising way — the transcendentalist pattern exemplified by Emerson.

WHEN just out of Harvard, Thoreau came under the powerful sway of Emerson's mind and did his formative thinking as a member of the Concord group of transcendentalists. He eventually liberated himself, however, from Emerson's influence, and at no time was he taken in by the transcendentalist excesses of the Concord group or by the millennial dreams that grew thick as huckleberries on the Concord bushes.

The sources of strength in his thinking came rather from other strains — an absorption with the Greek classics, a prolonged study of the Oriental teachings, the Graeco-British tradition of individualism, the nature-worship of the French and German philosophers and the English romantic poets, and finally a conscious modeling upon the way of life of the American Indians.

But Thoreau was not one to be too

deeply influenced. He was impervious to anything that did not fit into that continual quest for a practical solution of the problems of his own individual life which he called his philosophy. But implicit in his highly personal essays and nature soliloquies and journal entries is a devastating attack upon every dominant aspect of American life in its first flush of industrial advance — the factory system, the corporations, business enterprise, acquisitiveness, the vandalism of natural resources, the vested commercial and intellectual interests, the cry for expansion, the clannishness and theocratic smugness of New England society, the herd-mindedness of the people, the unthinking civic allegiance they paid to an opportunist and imperialist government.

He despised everything derivative and secondary. His criticism of American society sprang from the rebellion of the pioneer spirit. For he was seeking on an intellectual and moral frontier the zest and immediacy of the original pioneer effort and protesting passionately against the cultural crudity and the materialism of the pioneer in an industrial age. He rejected the factory system because it meant the exploitation of others; he rejected the cult of success and the Puritan creed of persistent work because it meant the exploitation of oneself. His economics anticipated Ruskin's by defining the cost of a thing as the amount of life that has to be exchanged for it; his aesthetics anticipated William Morris's by declaring that no beauty can exist in commodities that does not flow from a creativeness in the lives of those who fashion them. He recounts in *Walden* (1854) a two-year experiment in living in a hut in the woods, stripping the husk of civilization to the core, and setting up his own economy of wants and satisfactions. He found that the economic

system was making unreasonable demands on him, and so he proceeded to sabotage it, entering upon a conscientious withdrawal of efficiency which was none the less earnest because it was restricted to his own life. Similarly he sabotaged the government by refusing to pay taxes, and he spent a night in the village jail as an exultant political prisoner. His essay "Civil Disobedience" (1849) is a sharp statement of the duty of resistance to governmental authority when it is unjustly exercised; read by Gandhi in 1907, it became the foundation of the Indian civil disobedience movement. Thoreau's three speeches on John Brown (1859–1860; republished in Vol. X of the *Collected Works*) extol his insurrectionary attempt at Harpers Ferry and denounce the shortsighted coercion of the government that martyred him.

As a social critic Thoreau was uncompromising: his thought was tighter than Emerson's, less optimistic, less given to the resolution of opposites. It was a taut, astringent rejection of everything, that could not pass the most exacting tests of the individual life. In that sense there was something of the nihilist about Thoreau, and his thought effected an almost Nietzschean transvaluation of values.

But his hermit-like individualism may easily be overemphasized, just as his absorption with nature has been overemphasized. Both must be seen as part of a rebellion against the oversocialized New England town, in which the individual was being submerged, and against the factory system which saw nature only as so much raw material and sought to subdue it to the uses of profit. He was not so limited as to believe that the individual could by his own action stem the heedless onrush of American life, or succeed wholly in rechanneling it; yet, being a transcendentalist, he believed that a sharp moral protest such as that of John Brown, once clearly made, is ultimately irresistible. While he regarded individual development as the only aim of society, and the individual's moral sense as the only test and ultimately the only safeguard of institutions, he did not envisage the individual as the necessary cadre of society. "To act collectively is according to the spirit of our institutions," he wrote in *Walden*, and he follows this with a plea to extend the social services of the community and to make every New England village the basis of a venture in adult education. Nor did he wholly turn his back on the machine as an instrument of production: his emphasis was rather on its cultural consequences in his own day.

It was one of his characteristic paradoxes that the man who could solemnly call his fellow-townsmen together to read them a protest against the imprisonment of John Brown or the return of a fugitive slave could also profess an unconcern with most of the burning political issues of the day, and insist that his business was not to change the world but to solve the problem of living in it. He could say: "God does not sympathize with the popular causes," and at the same time have so deep a sense of the relation between a great culture and the common concerns of life that he has come down as perhaps the leading American nativist; commenting on the fact that no literature had yet grown up around "the Man of the Age, come to be called workingman," he remarks that "none yet speaks to his condition, for the speaker is not yet in his condition." It was his tragedy to be forced by the crudities of an expanding capitalism into a revulsion against society and its institutions that has until recently obscured the real force of his social thought. But there is about that thought a spare and canny strength and a quality of being unfooled that will survive even such a tragedy.

Heinz Eulau: WAYSIDE CHALLENGER: SOME REMARKS ON THE POLITICS OF HENRY DAVID THOREAU

Heinz Eulau has served with the Department of Justice, has been an editor of the New Republic, *and is now on the faculty of Stanford University. Among his books is a study of* Class and Party in the Eisenhower Years.

This paper is one of the few detailed and critical analyses of Thoreau's political ideas. Professor Eulau believes that Thoreau, despite the fact that he once said, "To act collectively is according to the spirit of our institutions," is an intransigent individualist, more the complete liberal than Max Lerner would allow. The outstanding defect of liberalism in America has been its "failure to come to grips with the distinction between morality and moral realism." A vital element of the politician's art, the "engineering of consent," depends upon the arrangement of compromise. But these liberals, of whom Thoreau is a prime example, cannot discern the difference between compromise as giving in to expediency and compromise as a mutual promise, a process of creative bargaining.

To act upon Thoreau's doctrine of civil disobedience can lead to ambiguous consequences; one may be moved by the pressure of events to the position that the end justifies the means, may cross the line — never clearly defined — between peaceful resistance to the enforcement of a law and actions which are flagrant violations of law. This Thoreau himself did when he fiercely defended John Brown's raid on Harpers Ferry. For righteous indignation is a dangerous mood; overprovoked, it can easily revert to purblind wrath. Today, tensions created by Vietnam, to so many the unintelligible war, and the increasing violence of racial conflict make it as difficult as it was in the decade before the Civil War to maintain a proper balance between the principle that government should be by the consent of the governed, and its corollary: that minorities — or any individual — may on moral grounds choose to disobey some law.

MODERN American Liberalism prides itself on being critical in spirit and pragmatic in method. Yet, if it has inherited anything from a less enlightened past, it is an attitude of self-righteous indignation which can see good only as good and bad only as bad. The logic of this morality is simple enough, but its consequences are paradoxical. Instead of fostering its central value, respect for the uniqueness and personality of the individual, liberalism succumbs to an ethical absolutism. Devoid of imaginative sympathy, it cannot understand that other creeds may have values at least comparable to its own. Liberalism then tends to become an affair of mere pronunciamento and simple magic formula. It seeks to counter the truths and perfections of its enemies by furnishing its own set of truths and perfections.

This paradox is due, I believe, to liberalism's failure to come to grips with the distinction between morality and moral realism. Moral realism, as here used, does not mean knowledge of good and bad, but knowledge of the ambiguities and anomalies of living the moral life. In contrast to morality, moral realism is aware of the possibility of good or bad consequences not as polar opposites, but of the possibility of "good-and-bad" consequences as ambivalent unities. Inasmuch as liberalism derives its values from moral realism, it has to accept ambivalence as necessary.

It is symptomatic of this dilemma, if a dilemma it is, that liberalism allows itself to be challenged by the metaphysical notion of individual moral conscience as a valid axiom of democratic politics. It suggests, in part at least, why Henry David Thoreau, though standing pretty much by the wayside of American

From Heinz Eulau, "Wayside Challenger: Some Remarks on the Politics of Henry David Thoreau," *Antioch Review*, Vol. IX (Winter 1949–1950), pp. 509–22. Reprinted by permission of the *Antioch Review*.

life, is as germane today as he ever was in the development of political thought. The one hundredth anniversary of his essay, "Civil Disobedience," is therefore only a fortuitous occasion to write about him. More pertinent, it seems, are the critical implications of his political ideas, absurd and inconsistent as they may appear.

It is unfair, perhaps, to judge Thoreau's political philosophy by present-day standards. Yet, it is necessary to do so because some recent interpreters have tried, in vain I think, to make Thoreau palatable to liberalism by reading their own preferences into his writings. But even if they seek to strike a balance, the end effect of their expositions is tortuous. Max Lerner, for instance, writes inaccurately, I believe, that Thoreau's individualism should be seen as part of "a rebellion against the oversocialized New England town, in which the individual was being submerged. . . . He was not so limited as to believe that the individual could by his own action stem the heedless onrush of American life, or succeed wholly in rechanneling it." Similarly, Townsend Scudder states that "though so intense an individualist, Thoreau favored the ideal of communal living as in keeping with the spirit of America." Significantly, Lerner, Scudder as well as F. O. Mathiessen repeat, by way of evidence, a single passage from Thoreau's *Walden* — "to act collectively is according to the spirit of our institutions." The bulk of proof is, in fact, on the other side. Even Vernon Parrington, whose progressivist bias is rarely concealed, recognized that Thoreau "could not adopt the cooperative solution." Thoreau refused to join Brook Farm because, in his own words, he "would rather keep a bachelor's hall in hell than go to board in heaven."

Thoreau does not give much comfort to those who seek to prove a point. But it should be remembered that *Walden,* his most famous and widely read book, does not alone represent his ideas. For an understanding of his politics, "Civil Disobedience" as well as the less-known and less-read essays, "Slavery in Massachusetts" (1854) and "A Plea for Captain John Brown" (1859), are of at least equal importance. They leave little doubt that Thoreau's whole political philosophy was based on the theoretical premise of individual conscience as the only true criterion of what is politically right and just. It was the very perfection of his belief in the veracity of each man's soul and conscience as harbingers of some truth higher than human fiat that made inconsistency in his theory inevitable. Action from principle, he wrote in a prophetic sentence in "Civil Disobedience," "not only divides states and churches, it divides families; ay, it divides the *individual,* separating the diabolical in him from the divine." Within the short span of ten years, Thoreau, though holding to the same premise, would draw conclusions as opposite as passive resistance and violent action. Obviously, both his personality and ideas were complex. Any attempt to reduce them to simple, and hence simpleton, propositions is futile.

2

While the subsequent essays are significant because they prove, better than critical argument, that "action from principle" is a politically dangerous concept, "Civil Disobedience" is the most complete theoretical statement of Thoreau's basic assumptions. Because it expounded a queer doctrine, unlikely to make much of an impression on his contemporaries, Thoreau apparently elaborated his political premise more fully in "Civil Disobedience" than in the subsequent essays.

His starting point is the half-mocking, half-serious observation that if Jefferson's motto — "that government is best which governs least" — were carried out, it would amount to "that government is best which governs not at all." Does this mean, as has been suggested, that Thoreau brought Jefferson's ideas to their logical conclusion? By no means. In placing the individual "above" the state, Jefferson attacked the autocratic state, not the democratic state which he did so much to bring about. If Thoreau went at all beyond Jefferson, it consisted in his attack on democracy. But, paradoxically, he attacked democracy not because it was strong; on the contrary, because it was weak. The American government, he wrote, "has not the vitality and force of a single living man; for a single man can bend it to his will." He refused to vote because he considered the democratic ballot an ineffective political instrument. His own contact with the government being limited to the annual *tête-à-tête* with the tax collector, his refusal to pay the poll tax loses some of its bravado. He did not really sacrifice much when he declared, somewhat grandiloquently, that he should not like to think he would ever have to rely on the protection of the state. Basically, Thoreau was the very opposite of Jefferson; he was as unpolitical as Jefferson was political. It is simply not conceivable to hear Jefferson say, as Thoreau said, "the government does not concern me much, and I shall bestow the fewest possible thoughts on it."

If Thoreau had let the matter rest at this point, his position would have been consistent. But as if he needed to test his own propositions, he would suddenly speak "practically and as a citizen, unlike those who call themselves no-government men." And as a citizen Thoreau demanded "not at once no government, but *at once* better government." Such a government would anticipate and provide for reform, cherish its "wise minority" and encourage its citizens "to be on the alert to point out its faults."

It appears that Thoreau could not fully discern that his metaphysical assumptions had to lead, almost necessarily, to ambiguous consequences when subjected to the test of practical politics. The essential weakness of the metaphysical premise is that it is absolutist as long as it deals with abstractions, just as it is relativistic when applied to unique and observable situations. Like his fellow idealists, Thoreau was incapable of recognizing those distinctions of degree which are politically decisive. He could not recognize them because he fell back, again and again, on the principle of individual conscience as the sole valid guide in political action. He realized only faintly that this principle was inherently deficient for political purposes, as when he said that while "all men recognize the right of revolution . . . , almost all say that such is not the case now." Individual conscience as a political principle was too obviously in conflict with the democratic principle of majority rule, even for Thoreau. But the rather dogmatic assertion, "there is but little virtue in the masses of men," was too hazardous in view of the manifest strength of the democratic faith of most men in his time. Thoreau's only way out was, once more, a paradox: "Any man more right than his neighbors constitutes a majority of one already."

Consequently, Thoreau had to postulate a (by democratic standards) curious distinction between law and right, with the explanation that one has to have faith in man, that each man can determine for himself what is right and just. Hence, no conflict is possible, so the argument goes, because law is law only if identical with right. Thoreau could not demonstrate, however, that there is, in case the majority is wrong, an objective criterion for assaying the correctness of an individual's or a minority's judgment.

He was content, therefore, with declaring war on the state in his own fashion:

It is not a man's duty as a matter of course, to devote himself to the eradication of any, even the most enormous wrong; he may still properly have other concerns to engage him; but it is his duty, at least, to wash his hands of it, and, if he gives it no thought longer, not to give it practically his support.

Great as his hurry seemed in "Civil Disobedience," Thoreau remained, in fact, unpolitical. Actually, he did not wish to be bothered at all with the obnoxious phenomenon of slavery. He had other affairs to attend to. "I came into this world," he concluded, "not chiefly to make this a good place to live in, but to live in it, be it good or bad." Joseph Wood Krutch has aptly described this kind of reasoning as Thoreau's "sometimes desperate casuistry."

3

The ideas expressed in "Civil Disobedience" fell into the Walden period (1845–1847) and are, to some extent, an early reaction to Thoreau's own dim sense of failure as a recluse from society. Existence at Walden Pond was an experiment for the purpose of finding reality. But subjectively real as life at Walden may have been, to judge from his famous report, it came to be unreal, apparently, when Thoreau was forced to compare it with the objective reality of the impending Mexican War which he encountered on his almost daily visits to town. There he would see his neighbors getting ready

for what seemed to him a hateful and stupid enterprise. Its effect could only be the extension of the unjust institution of slavery and of the slaveholders' power. Thoreau felt a deep personal disgrace in being associated with a government which was the slaves' government also. So deeply did he feel on the issue that he was ready to warn that "this people must cease to hold slaves, and to make war on Mexico, though it cost them their existence as a people." So great seemed the evil that there was no time to change the laws except by breaking them. Refusal to pay taxes was, in Thoreau's mind, "the definition of a peaceful revolution, if any such is possible." Otherwise, he continued, the conscience is wounded: "Through this wound a man's real manhood and immortality flow out, and he bleeds to an everlasting death. I see this blood flowing now."

All his protestations about "signing off" from human institutions to the contrary, "Civil Disobedience," in contrast to *Walden*, was a first indication of Thoreau's theoretical difficulties. It contained the seeds of its own denial, seeds which were fertilized by the untenable metaphysical premise of individual conscience as a criterion of collective action. In the very act of counseling and practicing individual resistance to and renunciation of government was implicit a growing sense of social responsibility which the hermit of Walden Pond could scarcely disclaim.

Thoreau was not, therefore, as *Walden* might suggest and some critics have said, an American exponent of the Rousseauist doctrine of the natural rights of man. His philosophy certainly lacked the liberating drive which Rousseau's individualism had in the eighteenth-century French context. Thoreau's individualism was, most interpreters agree, an inspired protest against the modern cult of progress, materialism and efficiency, with its deteriorating effect on the individual. But it was essentially out of date. Because it renounced industrialism rather than seeking to bring it under social control, Thoreau's individualism could not possibly find practical application. The moral and the morally real were at odds.

"Civil Disobedience" differed from *Walden* in another respect. *Walden* was the report of a highly personalized experience. And in spite of its persuasiveness, its almost egocentric individualism made communication difficult. Only the most liberal imagination can perceive it for what it was: namely, the attempt of a sensitive spirit to discover his own integrity and convey this discovery, not to be imitated literally — a mistake against which Thoreau himself explicitly warned, but to serve as a symbolic expression of man's need for finding his own integrity in whatever fashion seemed best. "I desire," he wrote, "that there be as many different persons in the world as possible; but I would have each one be very careful to find out and pursue *his own* way. . . ." As such, life at Walden Pond was a meaningful experiment, even though it was meaningless as a form of *social* living.

However, Thoreau's individualism was not simply, as Parrington remarked, "transcendental individualism translated into politics." His radicalism differed in more than degree from the innocuous, often opportunistic, politics of most Abolitionists. Their humanitarianism seemed all too sanguine to him. Were they not actually giving aid and comfort to the enemy by refusing to withdraw from political society altogether? In asking this question it must be admitted that Thoreau himself remained on a largely rhetorical level throughout his political life. Certainly, his refusal to pay the poll tax and being jailed for it was a frankly

ephemeral episode. But he found it increasingly necessary to communicate his ideas in a manner which would leave no doubt where he stood.

4

There is no better index of Thoreau's need to express himself unequivocally than the changing tenor of his humor. In "Civil Disobedience" it is of the most elusive variety. It was all too self-conscious and artificial to make it deeply personal and tragic as his human condition might have warranted. He shared his cell, "the whitest, most simply furnished, and probably the neatest apartment in town," with an alleged incendiary, "a first-rate fellow and a clever man." From the cell window, he reported, "I was an involuntary spectator and auditor of whatever was done and said in the kitchen of the adjacent village inn, — a wholly new and rare experience to me. It was a closer view of my native town. I was fairly inside of it." One cannot but feel that the atmosphere of mischief so created is more literary than political.

But the more Thoreau became involved in the slavery question in later years, the more his sense of frustration grew, the more scornful and vitriolic his humor would become. In "Slavery in Massachusetts" he would direct it at his Yankee audience. The soldier who lets himself be trained to return fugitive slaves to their masters "is a fool made conspicuous by a painted coat." Judges upholding the constitutionality of slavery "are merely inspectors of a pick-lock and murderer's tool." When he reads a newspaper defending the Fugitive Slave Law, he does it "with my cuffs turned up," and hears "the gurgling of the sewer through every column." It is a paper "picked out of the public gutters, the groggery, and the brothel, harmonizing with the gospel of the Merchants' Exchange."

Humor would finally give way to blasphemy in "A Plea for Captain John Brown." Though his counsel of passive, peaceful resistance had by then been replaced by the justification of violence, Thoreau's venom was that of a man close to despair. "Away with your broad and flat churches, and your narrow and tall churches," he cried; "take a step forward, and invent a new style of out-houses. Invent a salt that will save you, and defend your nostrils." He would excoriate the politicians as "office-seekers and speech-makers, who do not so much as lay an honest egg, but wear their breasts bare upon an egg of chalk."

Thoreau's desire to be understood by his fellow citizens is equally apparent if the symbols with which he appealed to his readers in "Civil Disobedience" are compared with those in "Slavery in Massachusetts." In the earlier essay he is preoccupied with Right, Truth and Justice. It is never quite clear whether he regarded passive resistance as a virtuous political goal, an end in itself, or whether he thought of it as the most effective means to abolish slavery. If the latter, he obscured his thinking pretty successfully. While a superb exposition of nonviolent resistance as a political instrument, the language used in "Civil Disobedience" does not indicate that Thoreau was particularly anxious to protest against the evil of slavery.

Indeed, it was not till the surrender by Massachusetts of the fugitive Negro Thomas Sims in 1851, an event which struck him as a "moral earthquake," and again of the Negro Anthony Burns in 1854, that Thoreau's anger was sufficiently aroused to make him abandon the convenient obscurantisms of the political idealists. No longer was the slavery issue a remote question which only incidentally annoyed him. His own state, Massachusetts, had violated a sacred trust when it returned these Negroes into slavery. Thoreau would now resort to patriotic sentiments in order to make his plea effective. "Every man in Massachusetts capable of the sentiment of patriotism," he wrote, must have had his own experience of "having suffered a vast and indefinite loss." And what was this loss which yesterday's anarchist felt so surprisingly? "At last it occurred to me that what I had lost was a country. . . . The remembrance of my country spoils my walk. My thoughts are murder to the State, and involuntarily go plotting against her."

This does not mean, of course, that Thoreau had abandoned his deep conviction that individual conscience is the safest guide in human affairs. It only means that, as time went on and the demands of politics required greater sophistication, Thoreau became somewhat more realistic. It was simply a matter of tactics if, as in "Slavery in Massachusetts," he identified individual conscience with the "laws of humanity," or, as in "A Plea for Captain John Brown," with "respect for the Constitution." Here he used catch-phrases which could be more easily grasped by the average citizen than metaphysical abstractions. But his attempt to make out of John Brown "a transcendentalist above all, a man of ideas and principles," did not quite come off. It merely showed that Thoreau knew as little about Brown as about slavery, and that he was projecting his metaphysical notions on a situation which hardly called for them.

5

As has been mentioned, in spite of the apparent urgency of his argument in "Civil Disobedience," Thoreau had experienced the Mexican War and its implications for the slavery question as a fairly remote conflict. But with the passage of the Fugitive Slave Law in 1850 it became evident, even to a political hermit like Thoreau, that continued detachment from affairs of state would not avert the threat to his personal liberty which the law implied. The state, he now discovered, "has fatally interfered with my lawful business." "Slavery in Massachusetts" was, therefore, as outspoken a piece of indignation as "Civil Disobedience" had been casual. He bade farewell to the pipedream of a state which would permit a few people, who so desired, to live aloof from it, "not meddling with it, nor embraced by it." He had never respected the government, he said, but "I had foolishly thought that I might manage to live here, minding my private affairs, and forget it." Thoreau now dropped the role of the bohemian anarchist who could wash his hands of society's "dirty institutions," as he had called them in *Walden*. Before, he admitted, he had dwelt in the illusion that "my life passed somewhere only *between* heaven and hell, but now I cannot persuade myself that I do not dwell *wholly* within hell."

Moreover, his rebellion was no longer a matter of denials alone. He still fulminated against majority rule, but a new line of thought occupied him. It would be too simple to say that a democratic faith emerged, but Thoreau's attack on existing institutions is certainly not that of the vociferous anti-democrat of "Civil Disobedience." As against judges deciding questions involving slaves, Thoreau would now "much rather trust the sentiment of the people. In their vote you would get something of value, at least, however small." It was no longer the state in the abstract, but the State of Massachusetts in the concrete which he attacked. He would recognize the possibility of a government which is worth fighting for. "Show me a free state, and a court truly of justice, and I will fight for them, if need be . . . ," he proclaimed;

"it is not an era of repose. We have used up all our inherited freedom. If we would save our lives, we must fight for them."

"Slavery in Massachusetts" was not a theoretical exercise in political philosophy. It concentrated its verbal fire on an evil situation. But it is indicative of Thoreau's political immaturity that he now went so far as to join the militant abolitionists in advocating the secession of Massachusetts from the union with the slave states. He was apparently quite unaware of the possibility that the consequences of such action might accentuate the evil which he sought to remedy. That is, permit slavery to continue unopposed elsewhere. In addition, he still confused what seemed to him the iniquity of law with the legal process itself. And though he spoke of breaking the law, of boycotting proslavery newspapers, of ousting ignorant politicians and seceding from the Union, it remains unclear just what specific political means Thoreau considered appropriate to achieve his objectives. He had almost given up passive resistance, but he had not completely accepted majority rule.

With all its new affirmations, "Slavery in Massachusetts" did not answer the question which is central from the point of view of political theory — whether the practicality of political concepts can be assessed by any kind of objectively rational standard. It seems that Thoreau was neither willing nor able to develop such a criterion. Not even "truth" would serve that purpose. Truth, he wrote in "Civil Disobedience," "is always in harmony with herself, and is not concerned chiefly to reveal the justice that may consist with wrong-doing." In other words, the consequences of an act are separable and, indeed, must be separated from its nature. Even truth is thus reduced to being a matter of individual taste. Thoreau admitted the existence of other truths, but being altogether personal and private they did not permit contact or comparison with each other. As so many of his concepts, his truth is paradoxical. His moral absolutism, being so individualized, becomes relativistic. It is not surprising to find, therefore, that Thoreau envisaged various hierarchial levels of political evaluation. "Seen from a lower point of view," he wrote, "the Constitution, with all its faults, is very good; the law and the courts are very respectable; even this State and this American government are, in many respects, very admirable, and rare things, to be thankful for, such as a great many have described them; but seen from a point of view a little higher, they are what I have described them; seen from a higher still, and the highest, who shall say what they are, or that they are worth looking at or thinking of at all?"

Paradox may serve the purpose of literary construction. In political theory it is self-defeating. Inasmuch as Thoreau's anarchism followed from the doctrine of the individual's duty to his conscience alone, it should lead to at least some mutual tolerance as an avenue to human cooperation. But Thoreau would carry the matter to absurdity. In a sentence remindful of the vicarious a-moralism of the later social Darwinians he wrote:

I am not responsible for the successful working of the machinery of society. . . . I perceive that, when an acorn and a chestnut fall side by side, the one does not remain inert to make way for the other, but both obey their own laws, and spring and grow and flourish as best they can, till one, perchance, overshadows and destroys the other. If a plant cannot live according to its nature, it dies; and so a man.

6

It is quite clear that Thoreau's mind was totally closed to the democratic conception of politics as a never-ending process of compromise and adjustment. As a matter of fact, if the politics of "action from principle," with its insistence on ends, is shorn of metaphysics, it appears as little more than the old and familiar doctrine that the end justifies the means. Comparison of "Civil Disobedience" and "A Plea for Captain John Brown" underlines the fact that in Thoreau's mind both passive resistance and violent action were *right* if employed toward the accomplishment of ends whose truth is predicated on the complete assumption of responsibility by the individual for his acts.

Just as nonviolent resistance as an instrument of politics is proper if the state interferes with an individual's principles, so violence can be justified. Given Thoreau's moral intransigence, it is not surprising to find that he would round out his basic position by eulogizing an event which only the most rabid Abolitionists supported as politically justifiable. John Brown, Thoreau came to believe, was not only right in holding that a man has "a perfect right to interfere by force with the slaveholder, in order to rescue the slave"; but the doctrine that the end justifies the means was given explicit expression: "I shall not be forward to think him mistaken in his method who quickest succeeds to liberate the slave." The decisive question, Thoreau finally felt, was not "about the weapon, but the spirit in which you use it." And he would write in his *Journals*: "I do not wish to kill nor to be killed, but I can foresee circumstances in which both these things would be by me unavoidable."

Actually, however, "A Plea for Captain John Brown" was concerned with the slavery issue only indirectly. Thoreau undoubtedly felt its iniquity and the urgency of its solution most intensely, but his primary concern was again with justice and injustice, with principle and expediency, with truth and falsehood. "A Plea for Captain John Brown" is therefore more closely related to "Civil Disobedience" than to "Slavery in Massachusetts." It differed, however, from his first political essay in that Thoreau had abandoned his earlier quietist position. Violence was in the air. Almost everywhere in the nation men were girding themselves for the great conflict which would soon disrupt the Union. While it may have been his intention merely to bring his disagreement with the moderate Abolitionists into sharper focus by advocating violence before the peaceful alternatives had been exhausted, the end effect of "A Plea for Captain John Brown" was the admission of an inveterate moralist that violence can only be combatted by violence.

It is symptomatic of his greater sense of realism that the government did not seem weak any longer as it had in "Civil Disobedience" ten years before. "When a government puts forth its strength on the side of injustice, as ours to maintain slavery and kill the liberators of the slave," he wrote, "it reveals itself a merely brute force, or worse, a demoniacal force. It is the head of the Plug-Uglies. It is more manifest than ever that tyranny rules. I see this government to be effectually allied with France and Austria in oppressing mankind." The government, he continued, is "a semi-human tiger or ox stalking over the earth, with its heart taken out and the top of its brain shot away."

Thoreau could no longer subscribe to the quietist doctrine of "Civil Disobedience" with its counsel of escape. He fiercely excoriated all those who adhered to a nonviolent solution of social conflict. "What sort of violence is that," he now asked, "which is encouraged, not by soldiers, but by peaceable citizens, not so much by laymen as by ministers of the Gospel, not so much by the fighting sects as by the Quakers, and not so much by the Quaker men as by the Quaker women?" Here Thoreau squarely faced the question of resistance by force which modern pacifism, confronted with the infamies of totalitarian terror and violence, slave labor and concentration camps, fails to answer. Here, in essence, he returned to the age-old concept of the "just war," which modern quietists refuse to acknowledge. John Brown would "never have anything to do with any war," Thoreau intimated, "unless it were a war for liberty," expressing an opinion since challenged by competent historians.

In John Brown, Thoreau had found the man of principle whom he had anticipated in "Civil Disobedience," the man "who is a *Man*, and, as my neighbor says, has a bone in his back which you cannot pass your hand through!" That this abstract man of principle had changed from the passive resister envisaged in 1849 into the violent and very real actionist of 1859 suggests that Thoreau had become aware of the futility of peaceful disobedience as much as he was oblivious of the dangers inherent in the idea of "action from principle."

Thoreau's conversion to violence as a legitimate means in the social conflict cannot be attributed to a purely rational thought process. The fervor of his eulogy betrays its emotional content. He identified himself with Brown so much that he experienced the latter's ordeal after the disastrous incident at Harpers Ferry as a personal tragedy. "I put a piece of paper and a pencil under my pillow," he wrote, "and when I could not sleep I wrote in the dark." Brown had the stuff heroes are made of. "No doubt," Thoreau postulated, "you can get more in your market for a quart of milk than for a quart of blood, but that is not the market that heroes carry their blood to." As if he felt a sense of personal guilt about his own irresponsibility in days gone by, Thoreau expressed his admiration for Brown because he "did not wait till he was personally interfered with or thwarted in some harmless business before he gave his life to the cause of the oppressed." And it is more than obvious that Thoreau rationalized the a-moral consequences of his new departure when he stated that people at most criticized Brown's tactics and then added: "Though you may not approve of his method or his principles, recognize his magnanimity."

Significantly, too, the eulogy in defense of John Brown was not characterized by so transitory a feeling as that which attended the experience of his own imprisonment. On being released from jail after having refused to pay the poll tax, he had joined a huckleberry party in the highest hills, where "the State was nowhere to be seen." Many weeks after his passionate plea, he noted in his *Journals* that it was hard for him to see the beauty of a remarkable sunset when his mind "was filled with Captain Brown. So great a wrong as his fate implied overshadowed all beauty in the world." Bronson Alcott reported in his *Journals* that Thoreau had called on him because he thought that "someone from the North should see Gov. Wise, or write concerning Capt. Brown's character and motives, to influence the Governor in his favor."

7

It has not been my intention to disparage Thoreau's reputation as the outstanding American spokesman for those human values which the empty materialism of our culture so readily relegates to the limbo of sanctimonious oratory. Criticism of his political theory cannot possibly deprive Thoreau's words of that immortality with which his moral sincerity, his spiritual courage and his sense of genuine inquiry have endowed it. His ideas are living ideas for the very reason that he lived them, day in and day out. The acidity of his attack and the persistence of his independence are admired and emulated by thousands who grope for a way to withstand the seemingly invincible force of personal and social maladjustments. As his friend and earliest biographer F. H. Sanborn has said, "The haughtiness of his independence kept him from a thousand temptations that beset men of less courage and self-denial."

But I also believe that those who neglect and even deny the ambiguities and paradoxes of Thoreau's moral intransigence misunderstand the real challenge of his politics. They overlook the essential assumptions underlying his advice of civil disobedience. Hence, they are at a loss in explaining his repudiation of his own advice and his justification of violent resistance.

Thoreau's philosophy should warn us of the dilemma into which he fell and from which he could not escape because he returned time and again, to individual conscience as the "ultimate reality." His thought was full of ambiguity and paradox, and he did not realize sufficiently how contradictory and, in fact, dangerous the moral can be. Granted, he had no fear of consequences in disregarding the law. But, as Pascal observed, "he who would act the angel acts the brute." There is no virtue in accepting the consequences of an act because the premise from which they flow might be essentially good. Thoreau's politics suggests that it is a small step, indeed, from insistence on the principle of morality to insistence on the principle of expediency.

Martin Luther King, Jr.:
A LEGACY OF CREATIVE PROTEST

The Reverend Martin Luther King, Jr., a leader of the civil rights movement, was awarded the Nobel Peace Prize in 1964. He once said, "From my Christian background I gained my ideals and from Gandhi my operational technique." Like Gandhi, though, he was early influenced by reading Thoreau, to whom he here pays tribute.

Martin Luther King believed Gandhi's statement: "My creed of non-violence is an extremely active force." Gandhi was assassinated. The truth of the Indian leader's statement was reaffirmed when, on April 4, 1968, King too was murdered.

During my early college days I read Thoreau's essay on civil disobedience for the first time. Fascinated by the idea of refusing to cooperate with an evil system, I was so deeply moved that I re-read the work several times. I became convinced then that non-cooperation with evil is as much a moral obligation as is cooperation with good. No other person has been more eloquent and passionate in getting this idea across than Henry David Thoreau. As a result of his writings and personal witness we are the heirs of a legacy of creative protest. It goes without saying that the teachings of Thoreau are alive today, indeed, they are more alive today than ever before. Whether expressed in a sit-in at lunch counters, a freedom ride into Mississippi, a peaceful protest in Albany, Georgia, a bus boycott in Montgomery, Alabama, it is an outgrowth of Thoreau's insistence that evil must be resisted and no moral man can patiently adjust to injustice.

From *Thoreau in Our Season,* ed. John H. Hicks (Amherst, 1966), p. 13. Reprinted by permission of the University of Massachusetts Press.

William Stuart Nelson: THOREAU AND AMERICAN NON-VIOLENT RESISTANCE

William Stuart Nelson has served as president of two universities, Shaw and Dillard, and as dean of the School of Religion at Howard University. One of the books he has published is Bases of World Understanding.

Dean Nelson calls Thoreau's doctrine one of "non-violent resistance." "As such, it includes the assertion of the right of conscience in the presence of the rule of law. It is an appeal beyond government to the character of those whom the government purports to represent." And, to be properly understood, it must be placed within its context — Thoreau's revolt against materialism in all forms.

Eulau found this doctrine, as expressed in "Civil Disobedience," incompatible with Thoreau's subsequent defense of John Brown, who, having been convicted for the seizure of the federal arsenal at Harpers Ferry "of murder, criminal conspiracy, and treason against the Commonwealth of Virginia," was duly hanged. Brown thought himself a martyr, as willing "to die for God's eternal truth on the scaffold as in any other way." And Emerson acclaimed John Brown a "new saint, who will make the gallows glorious like the cross." Nelson appears to believe that there is no incompatibility: Thoreau, he says, "saw through the crust of John Brown's violence."

IT IS YET to dawn fully upon the participants in sit-ins, freedom rides and other recent forms of non-violent resistance in the United States how deeply indebted they are to Henry David Thoreau. Thoreau's name is mentioned upon occasion. Martin Luther King recalls that early in the 1955 bus boycott of Montgomery, Alabama, he reflected on Thoreau's essay on "Civil Disobedience" and was convinced that in Montgomery he and his followers were simply making clear, in the spirit of Thoreau, that they could no longer co-operate with an evil system.

Participants in this non-violent movement acknowledge a profound indebtedness to Mohandas K. Gandhi. Those who have not read the following words of Gandhi would profit in so doing:

Why, of course, I read Thoreau. I read *Walden* first in Johannesburg in South Africa in 1906 and his ideas influenced me greatly. I adopted some of them and recommended the study of Thoreau to all my friends who were helping me in the cause of Indian independence. Why, I actually took the name of my movement from Thoreau's essay, "On the duty of Civil Disobedience," written about eighty years ago. Until I read that essay I never found a suitable English translation for my Indian word, *Satyagraha*. You remember that Thoreau invented and practised the idea of civil disobedience in Concord, Massa-

From *Thoreau in Our Season*, ed. John H. Hicks (Amherst, 1966), pp. 14–18. Reprinted by permission of the University of Massachusetts Press.

chusetts, by refusing to pay his poll tax as a protest against the United States government. He went to jail too. There is no doubt that Thoreau's ideas greatly influenced my movement in India.[1]

The right to disobey government has been defended in literature and in practice for thousands of years, but Americans engaged in or confronted by a civil resistance movement must above all understand Thoreau. He conceded that government is a present necessity but held that governments by their very nature are prone to err. The best of them are supported by majorities, indicating a victory of numbers and not necessarily of justice. Law makers, as Thoreau observed, too frequently serve the state with their heads and often unintentionally serve the devil. What place, we may then inquire, is left in such a government for conscience? If it is desirable to develop a respect for law, it is essential to cultivate a respect for conscience.

A genuine non-violent movement, therefore, includes the assertion of the right of conscience in the presence of the rule of law. It is an appeal beyond government to the character of those whom the government purports to represent.

Such an appeal, if it is responsible, has its laws. Civil resistance is not necessarily invoked against every law which is regarded as bad. It is obvious that a man cannot give himself to the eradication of every wrong however great. He can, of course, disassociate himself from it. Against what wrong of government, then, should he oppose his conscience? In "Civil Disobedience" Thoreau has a formula: "If the injustice is part of the necessary friction of the machine of government, let it go, let it go: perchance it

will wear smooth — certainly the machine will wear out . . . but if it is of such a nature that it requires you to be an agent of injustice to another, then, I say, break the law. Let your life be a counter friction — friction to stop the machine. What I have to do is to see, at any rate, that I do not lend myself to the wrong which I condemn."

Civil disobedience requires also on the part of the resister the willing subjection to the penalty exacted by the law. As Thoreau states, "Under a government which imprisons any unjustly the true place for a just man is also in prison." If the place of the fugitive slave in Massachusetts is in prison, then the only place for her free and just citizens is also in the prisons. This is in token of respect for law as law. Moreover, it gives maximum force to protest, for as Thoreau points out a just minority is irresistible when it acts with its whole weight. The state will not place or keep all just men in prison. Rather than this, it will abandon its evil practice.

The discussion of the civil disobedience aspect of non-violence and non-violent resistance is of greatest importance, but it would be extremely shortsighted and superficial to conclude that the meaning of non-violence is exhausted merely by such a discussion. It is likewise unfortunate to separate Thoreau's doctrine of civil disobedience from other profound manifestations of his spirit. To persist in so doing is to miss the total message which he so forcefully epitomizes. It is only in the grasping of this total message that Negroes might possibly guarantee the fulfillment of Gandhi's fateful prophecy, namely, that it might be through them that the unadulterated message of non-violence would be made available to the world.

The roots of Thoreau's concept of civil

[1] Quoted by George Hendrick, "Influence of Thoreau and Emerson on Gandhi's Satyagraha," *Gandhi Marg.*, III (July, 1959), 166.

resistance were deep. As a Transcendentalist he had turned away from economic royalism and was convinced that the purest insight commonly was not to be found in the person who accumulated property. His poverty he wore as a badge of honor and he preached eloquently against materialism, the disease of his century, reminding men that they err in laying up treasures which moths corrupt.

For him, living was the precious goal and the cost of a thing was "the amount of life it requires to be exchanged for it immediately and in the long run." Rebelling against acquisition, he was happy in the gift to him by the gods of years without an encumbrance. He was willing to live so Spartan-like as to put to flight all that was not life. He journeyed to Walden Pond not, as some may think, to flee from life but in the midst of this apparent privation to find it. One is reminded of Gandhi in our own time, who insisted that in the spirit of this self-denial he must reduce himself to zero. The Christ, the Buddha — all those who have found the secret of living in its noblest flowering — have seen the wisdom of finding the self by losing it. It cannot be expected that non-violent movements will be completely manned by such spirits as these. At the center, however, there must be those selfless, disinterested standard-bearers for whom fulness of life exists apart from material possessions.

There is a further quality without which no truly non-violent movement can be built. It is compassion — not simply sorrow for the suffering man but identification with him. This is the quality that led Gandhi to adopt his scant attire when he saw a woman in her one remaining sari, the remnant of a once adequate garment, and to declare that he would wear this minimum attire until somehow no longer would a woman of India be forced to such an embarrassing estate; or led Gandhi, when he could not abolish untouchability, to adopt an untouchable as his daughter and often to elect to live among untouchables.

Some may find it difficult to associate this quality with Thoreau. It was nonetheless present. His identification with the evil linked to the extension of slavery led him to prison; his unity in spirit with John Brown enabled Thoreau to defend him in the face of bitter hostility and threatened violence. Most men saw and judged John Brown from the outside. Thoreau knew and felt him from within. When the village postmaster was reported to have said of John Brown, "He died as the fool dieth," Thoreau said he should have been answered as follows: "He did not live as the fool liveth, and he died as he lived." Thoreau declared also: "It galls me to listen to the remarks of craven-hearted neighbors who speak disparagingly of Brown because he resorted to violence, resisted the government, threw his life away! — what way have they thrown their lives, pray? — neighbors who would praise a man for attacking singly an ordinary band of thieves or murderers. Such minds are not equal to the occasion. They preserve the so-called peace of their community by deeds of petty violence every day. . . . So they defend themselves and their hen roosts, and maintain slavery." Thoreau continued: "There sits a tyrant holding fettered four millions of slaves. Here comes their heroic liberator; if he falls, will he not still live?"

Thoreau saw through the crust of John Brown's violence, a violence which Brown had learned from thousands of years of pagan and Christian history and the practice of his own time. Thoreau, penetrating that crust, identified himself with the spirit of the man which sought the overthrow of an evil system.

The lesson here is that in a movement motivated by genuine non-violence, such as inspires the current resistance to racial injustice in America, men risk their lives not for beliefs but for *passionate* beliefs, beliefs in which intellectual accord has been deepened by spiritual identification.

These two threads — civil disobedience on the one hand and, on the other, capacity for divorcement from the material along with passionate identification with suffering — remained consistently interwoven throughout the life of Henry David Thoreau in spite of the urgings by others that he order his life otherwise. To illustrate, following the night in jail Thoreau completed his journey to the shoemaker interrupted by his arrest the day before. Having retrieved his shoe, he went huckleberrying. Emerson felt impatiently that Thoreau, instead of serving as the captain of huckleberry parties, should be employing his great gifts in leadership for all America. This, of course, would have proved a large responsibility even in Thoreau's and Emerson's time. Fortunately, Thoreau was not moved from his course. He remained true to himself. In our time, his life and thought, developed between and perhaps even during his jaunts through the woods in quest of huckleberries, move with increasing power upon America. Those who today assume the difficult role of removing certain of our country's weaknesses by non-violence, including civil disobedience, will do well to ponder Thoreau both as jail-goer and the voice of protest. Thoreau should also be remembered as one who resisted the temptation to permit things to ride in the saddle of his soul and who counted his life as none too precious a gift in testimony to his compassion for justice and for those who were willing to die in its behalf.

Suggestions for Additional Reading

The classic study of the Jacksonian era is, of course, Alexis de Tocqueville, *Democracy in America;* the preferred edition is by Phillips Bradley, (2 vols., New York, 1948). Two excellent contemporary interpretations of the period as a whole are Arthur M. Schlesinger, Jr., *The Age of Jackson* (Boston, 1945) and Marvin Meyers, *The Jacksonian Persuasion* (Stanford, Cal., 1957; 2nd ed., New York, 1960). Carl R. Fish, *The Rise of the Common Man* (New York, 1927) is a useful social history. Glyndon G. Van Deusen, *The Jacksonian Era* (New York, 1959) gives a comprehensive treatment of the political struggles of the period. For an interesting briefer account see the chapter entitled "Andrew Jackson and the Rise of Liberal Capitalism" in Richard Hofstadter, *The American Political Tradition and the Men Who Made It* (New York, 1948). The industrial changes during this time are conveniently summarized in the first four chapters of Thomas C. Cochran and William Miller, *The Age of Enterprise* (New York, 1942). The most perceptive detailed account of these momentous developments is George Rogers Taylor, *The Transportation Revolution — 1815–1860* (New York, 1951). Collections of writings about the period which are most helpful for an understanding of it are: Joseph L. Blau, *Social Theories of Jacksonian Democracy* (New York, 1954) and the two works (one of them in this series) by Edwin C. Rozwenc: *The Meaning of Jacksonian Democracy* (Boston, 1963) and *Ideology and Power in the Age of Jackson* (New York, 1964). Finally, John William Ward, *Andrew Jackson, Symbol for an Age* (New York, 1955) brilliantly depicts the climate of opinion in the only period of American history named for a man.

For the transcendentalist movement as a whole there is the relatively brief but highly suggestive account, "The Transcendental Mind," in volume two of Vernon L. Parrington's *Main Currents in American Thought* (New York, 1927). The best detailed and comprehensive study is F. O. Matthiessen, *American Renaissance: Art and Expression in the Age of Emerson and Whitman* (New York, 1941). Van Wyck Brooks, *The Flowering of New England* (New York, 1936) gives vivid sketches of the important members of the group in their local habitations; and Perry Miller's anthology *The American Transcendentalists, Their Prose and Poetry* (New York, 1957) is a good introduction to their own writings. On the philosophical side there is an excellent brief treatment in Herbert W. Schneider, *A History of American Philosophy* (New York, 1946; 2nd. ed. 1963). The best detailed analysis of Emerson's ideas is Stephen E. Whicher, *Freedom and Fate: An Inner Life of Ralph Waldo Emerson* (Philadelphia, 1953). Harold C. Goddard, *Studies in New England Transcendentalism* (New York, 1908) and Henry D. Gray, *Emerson* (Stanford, Cal., 1917) are also valuable studies of transcendentalism as a philosophy.

Among books which have sections or chapters that help to place the transcendentalist movement within the wider continuities of American cultural history are: Yehoshua Arieli, *Individualism and Nationalism in American Ideology* (Cambridge, Mass., 1964); Loren Baritz, *City on a Hill, A History of Ideas and Myths in America* (New York, 1964); Daniel Aaron, *Men of Good Hope: A Story of American Progressives* (New York, 1951); and especially Leo Marx's original and provocative work, *The Machine in the Garden: Technology and the Pastoral Ideal In America* (New York, 1964).

Individual transcendentalists have expressed their attitudes toward politics, reform movements, and commercial enterprise with vigor. See Emerson's essays on "Politics" and "New England Reformers" in *Essays: Second Series* (1844); "Historic Notes on Life and Letters in New England" and "Chardon Street Convention" in *Lectures and Biographical Sketches* (1883). This material and more is conveniently collected in *The Portable Emerson* (New York, 1946) with a valuable introduction by Mark Van Doren. Thoreau's *Walden* (1854) is a central document of transcendental opinion and should be read entire, with special emphasis on Chapters 1 and 2. From Thoreau's *Miscellanies* see "Paradise (to Be) Regained" (1843) and "Life without Principle" (1863).

Special studies that bear on this aspect of the subject are: Raymer McQuiston, *The Relation of Ralph Waldo Emerson to Public Affairs* (Lawrence, Kansas, 1923); Mildred Silver, "Emerson and the Idea of Progress," *American Literature,* 12 (1940), 1–19; Alexander C. Kern, "Emerson and Economics," *New England Quarterly,* 13 (1940), 678–696; Joseph W. Beach, "Emerson and Revolution," *University of Toronto Quarterly,* 3 (1934), 474–497; Wendell Glick, "Thoreau's Attack on Relativism" *Western Humanities Review,* 7 (1952–53), 35–42; F. B. Dedmond, "Thoreau and the Ethical Concept of Government" *The Personalist,* 36 (1955), 36–46; George Hendrick, "The Influence of 'Civil Disobe-

dience' on Ghandi's *Satyagraha*," *New England Quarterly,* 29 (1956), 462–471; Leo Stoller, *After Walden, Thoreau's Changing Views on Economic Man* (Stanford, Cal., 1957); Laurence Bowling "Thoreau's Social Criticism as Poetry," *Yale Review,* 55 (1965–66), 255–264; Arthur I. Lodu, "The Political Ideas of Theodore Parker," *Studies in Philology,* 33 (1941) 106–123. Other studies — some of the best — are to be found in four anthologies of critical writings on Emerson and Thoreau: *Emerson, a Collection of Critical Essays,* edited by Milton R. Konvitz and Stephen E. Whicher, (Englewood Cliffs, N. J., 1962); *Thoreau, A Century of Criticism,* edited by Walter Harding, (Dallas, Texas, 1954); *Thoreau, A Collection of Critical Essays,* edited by Sherman Paul, (Englewood Cliffs, N. J., 1962); *Thoreau in Our Season,* edited by John H. Hicks, (Amherst, Mass., 1966).

Acquaintance with individual transcendentalists as persons may best be begun by consulting their journals: *The Heart of Emerson's Journals,* edited by Bliss Perry, (Boston, 1926); *The Journals of Ralph Waldo Emerson,* an abridgement edited by Robert N. Linscott, (New York, 1960); *The Heart of Thoreau's Journals,* edited by Odell Shephard, (Boston, 1927); *The Journals of Bronson Alcott,* edited by Odell Shephard, (Boston, 1938). One of the many anthologies, *Selections from Ralph Waldo Emerson* (Boston, 1957), edited by Stephen E. Whicher, is arranged chronologically and draws heavily upon the journals and letters.

From among many biographical and critical studies — in addition to the book by Stephen Whicher previously mentioned — the following may be especially recommended: Bliss Perry, *Emerson Today* (Princeton, 1931), a brief book but filled with insight; Robert C. Pollock's brilliant study, "Ralph Waldo Emerson: The Single Vision," in *American Classics Reconsidered*, edited by Harold C. Gardiner, (New York, 1958); Ralph L. Rusk, *The Life of Ralph Waldo Emerson* (New York, 1949), the most detailed biography; Joseph Wood Krutch, *Thoreau* (New York, 1948), an exceptionally lucid analysis of transcendental thought; Sherman Paul, *The Shores of America: Thoreau's Inward Exploration* (Urbana, Ill., 1958); George F. Whicher, *Walden Revisited* (Chicago, 1945), brief but highly illuminating; Walter Harding, *The Days of Henry Thoreau* (New York, 1965), the latest and most scholarly account of his life; Odell Shephard, *Pedlar's Progress* (Boston, 1937), a full and scholarly tracing of the career of Bronson Alcott; Henry S. Commager, *Theodore Parker, Yankee Crusader* (Boston, 1936), a tribute to a Christian hero. Professor Commager has also edited *Theodore Parker: An Anthology* (Boston, 1960).

Utopian movements in America are surveyed in Francis T. Russell, *Touring Utopia: The Realm of Constructive Humanism* (New York, 1932); Alice Felt Tyler, *Freedom's Ferment* (Minneapolis, Minn., 1944) and Mark Holloway, *Heavens on Earth* (2nd. ed., New York, 1966). On Brook Farm in particular, consult Katherine Burton, *Paradise Planters: The Story of Brook Farm* (New York, 1939);

Edith R. Curtis, *A Season in Utopia* (New York, 1961); Lindsay Swift, *Brook Farm: Its Members, Scholars, and Visitors* (New York, 1900), encyclopedic and a trifle dull; John T. Codman, *Brook Farm: Historic and Personal Memoirs* (Boston, 1894); and Eliza P. Peabody, *Last Evening with Allston, and Other Papers* (Boston, 1886). An informative study of Fruitlands is by Clara E. Sears: *Bronson Alcott's Fruitlands* (Boston, 1915).

Full lists of writings dealing with individual authors may be found in the bibliography attached to Spiller, Thorp, Johnson, and Canby, *Literary History of the United States* (New York, 1948), the supplemental bibliography edited by Richard M. Ludwig (New York, 1959), and the annual volumes issued by the Modern Language Association and the *Annual Bibliography of English Language and Literature*.

Two pieces that would have been included, were there the space among these readings, as wryly humorous commentaries on the whole "revolt," one by an involuntary participant, the other by a present-day writer, are the slightly fictionalized account of Fruitlands by Louisa May Alcott, "Transcendental Wild Oats," from *Silver Pitchers* (1876), which is printed in the original edition of this volume, and E. B. White's essay "Walden," from *One Man's Meat* (New York, 1944).